The Digital Classroom

By: Brittany Washburn

TEACHERGOALS
PUBLISHING

THE DIGITAL CLASSROOM

Published by TeacherGoals Publishing, LLC Beech Grove, IN
www.teachergoals.com
Cover Designer: Tricia Fuglestad
Interior Designer: Heather Brown
Developmental and Line Editor: Kate Allyson
Copy Editor: Carrie Turner

Library of Congress Control Number: 2025935205
Paperback ISBN: 978-1-959419-32-7
ASIN: B0G26ZQDCV

First Printing: January 2026

The Digital Classroom

By: Brittany Washburn

TEACHERGOALS
PUBLISHING

Table of Contents

Introduction

The Evolving Landscape of Education and the Call for Digital Literacy

Many years ago, in a classroom filled with the hum of computers and the bright glow of monitors, I began my journey as a tech teacher. The year was 2012, and I was stepping into a world brimming with opportunity — teaching technology to enthusiastic grades K-5 students. The prospect was exciting, but what awaited me was more of an evolution than I had anticipated.

In the first year, I was eager and armed with a curriculum plan that was heavily centered around the basics: mastering Microsoft Word, designing with Paint, and crafting engaging slides in PowerPoint. The students would troop in, eyes filled with a mixture of curiosity and apprehension, hands tentatively touching the keyboards, and minds wondering about the magic these machines held.

However, by the second year, I noticed a shift. Outside the classroom, these kids were interacting with technology in ways I hadn't even imagined during my school days. They were swiping on tablets, playing interactive games, and even using voice-activated assistants. The traditional curriculum felt somewhat disconnected. Instead of being an exciting class, diving deep into the digital realm, we were just skimming the surface.

That's when the real transformation began. My second year marked the dawn of a new approach. Instead of just teaching my students about tech, I began teaching them through tech. We started projects that weren't just about using a tool but about creating something new and unique with it. The classroom became a hub of innovation. Students collaborated on digital storybooks, designed virtual art galleries, and even dabbled in basic coding exercises.

Gone were the days of passive learning. Each student became a creator, an innovator. Instead of asking, "How do I format this text?" they began pondering, "How can I use this tool to share my story?" or "What can I create that's never been made before?"

Those initial years weren't just a trajectory of teaching tech but a lesson in evolution, adaptability, and understanding the ever-shifting dynamics of the digital age. From hesitant typists to confident creators, the transformation of my students mirrored the very essence of the tech revolution: it's not just about tools, it's about the wonders we can achieve with them.

It wasn't just in the classroom that I made observations that led to my EdTech evolution.

Once, on a breezy afternoon about a decade ago, I found myself seated at a local café, sipping on my latte. Across from me, a tiny toddler was handed a tablet by her mother, presumably to keep her entertained. I observed, somewhat skeptically, expecting the child to merely tap randomly. To my astonishment, the little girl navigated the device with ease, swiping between apps and choosing her desired cartoons. I was taken aback. The era of intuitive technology literacy had dawned.

Over the years, I've had the privilege of watching these students, these tech-whisperers, grow and integrate into our educational spaces. It was as if they had an intrinsic bond with technology, like a sixth sense. They swiped and tapped with the same naturalness with which my generation turned pages of cherished storybooks or spun the dials of old radios. For these youngsters, the line between the physical and digital was beautifully blurred.

I remember a particular day in class when I introduced a new digital drawing tool, The Paper 53 tablet app. There was a buzz of excitement in the room, and as the students dove into the task, it hit me: the potential in front of me was monumental. Sarah, a quiet girl in the third row, used the tool to craft an intricate digital landscape, each pixel reflecting her understanding and creativity. Meanwhile, Jake, who often struggled with pen-and-paper tasks, was flourishing, turning lines and shapes into a story about space exploration.

It became abundantly clear that we weren't merely training tech-savvy students. This was about more than knowing which buttons to press. We were nurturing a generation ready to challenge, innovate, and shape the world. Their interactions with technology were profound; it wasn't just mindless clicking. They were at the cusp of questions that delved deep, theories that pushed boundaries, and creations that showcased their raw, brilliant potential.

The decade unfurled, bringing with it unparalleled shifts in educational paradigms. But amidst all the change, one thing remained constant: the gleam in the eyes of our students, ready to harness technology to paint their futures. They weren't just using tech; they were living it, molding it, and in many ways, teaching us about the vast landscapes of possibility it held. Every click, every swipe was a step towards a future painted in the vibrant colors of creativity and critical thinking. As an educator, I was both a witness and a guide on this incredible journey.

As the world becomes more digital by the second, it's our duty to ensure our kids don't just consume technology but use it to shape their futures and, in turn, the world. It's a thrilling journey, and I'm so excited to navigate this with you!

I want to take you on this journey to make your classroom more future-ready, and by the end of this book, I have some goals in mind for you. Let's explore them:

1. **Embracing Tech's Potential**: You're going to see that introducing tech in the classroom isn't about shiny new gadgets. No, it's a pathway. Through this book, I hope to show you how tech can be a golden ticket to fostering qualities like creativity, problem-solving,

and critical thinking in our students. If you've ever wondered why tech should have a seat in the educational realm, we'll unravel that mystery together.

2. **The Magic of the iTECH model**: You might have heard whispers about this in the educational corridors, but we're diving deep! By the time you turn that last page, you'll be well-versed in how to bring the iTECH model (Inspire, Try, Expand, Create, Huddle) to life in your classroom. We're talking about turning ordinary lessons into extraordinary learning experiences.

3. **Wielding Tech Tools Like a Pro**: Not all tech is made equal, especially when it comes to the classroom. We'll delve into various tools and strategies suitable for various subjects and age groups. Whether you teach math to first graders or history to fifth graders, there's something in store for everyone.

4. **Crafting Future-Ready Learning Spaces**: It's not just about having tech. It's about creating a space where tech meets purpose. We'll embark on a journey to design a classroom where every student feels seen, heard, and most importantly, empowered in their unique tech-driven learning journey.

5. **Evaluation and Evolution**: Once we've got all these cool tools and techniques in place, how do we know they're working? We'll venture into the realms of assessment and understand how to measure the impact of tech on our students. More importantly, we'll discuss how to refine and revamp based on what the data tells us.

6. **Never Stop Learning**: The tech world is like a river, always flowing, always changing. I'll guide you on how to stay afloat by constantly updating yourself. We'll discuss platforms, workshops,

and networking opportunities that keep you in the loop.

7. **Building Our Community**: Lastly, but perhaps most importantly, it's about building a community. Education is a shared journey, and when educators band together, magic happens. We'll explore how to collaborate, exchange ideas, and uplift one another. Together, we'll foster a community that champions empowerment, sharing, and forward-thinking.

So, whether you're a tech novice or a digital guru, there's a place for you in this narrative. Let's embark on this transformative journey and reshape the way we view education for our modern students. Ready? Let's dive in!

Section 1
Embracing Technology in Education

Chapter 1
Adventures in EdTech: My Journey Through Today's Classroom

Navigating the constantly changing world of educational technology feels like embarking on an expedition without a map. I remember the first time I watched in awe as students, using virtual reality (VR) and augmented reality (AR) headsets, strolled through ancient ruins and swam beside colorful fish in the deepest oceans. It's one thing to read about history or marine biology, but to 'live' it? That's magic. These tools are not just fancy gadgets, they're doorways to immersive, unforgettable learning experiences.

Then there's the rise of artificial intelligence (AI) in our classrooms. On a practical note, I saw how it transformed a friend's teaching experience. She once spent hours grading papers and identifying learning gaps. Now, with AI-driven tools, she gets insights at her fingertips. Her students receive personalized feedback and lessons tailored to their pace and style. It's like having a classroom assistant who knows every student's strengths and areas of growth.

Speaking of connections, the collaborative tools now available are revolutionizing group projects. Remember the days of passing notes and coordinating group meetings? Now, students from different corners of the world can brainstorm in real-time, share files, and even virtually 'high-five' on platforms designed specifically for classroom collaboration. It's a connected world, and our classrooms are a testament to that.

As I glanced at my smartphone one evening, I realized that these devices have done more than just change how we communicate; they've transformed learning itself. Students are no longer bound by the four walls of a classroom. With educational apps and the internet, the world is at their fingertips. Whether they're creating multimedia presentations or watching an instructional video, mobile learning is redefining the word classroom.

My Classroom Epiphany:
From Consumers to Creators

During my second year as a technology teacher, while prepping for my next class, a thought struck me—my students were brilliant at consuming content, but what about creating it? I envisioned them not just as learners, but as thinkers and problem-solvers who could harness technology to craft their own narratives.

It all started with an app. I stumbled upon a myriad of educational apps tailored to stir students' critical thinking. One, in particular, threw real-world scenarios at them, inviting solutions. Watching them brainstorm was like witnessing tiny sparks light up a room. It was fun, interactive, and made problem-solving less of a task and more of an exciting challenge.

Then, there was the day we took a dive into online collaboration. With platforms like Google Classroom and Padlet, my students connected with peers from continents away, weaving global stories and solving problems together. Their conversations brimmed with ideas, and their collaborative projects became melting pots of varied perspectives. Technology wasn't just a tool; it was a bridge, a connection, and a window to the world.

One day, while watching my niece play a video game, it dawned on me how schools could tap into this gaming passion. Enter gamification. Schools are now turning lessons into rewarding challenges, complete with badges, leaderboards, and playful competition. It's incredible how a touch of playful competition can ignite such enthusiasm in learning.

I began to sprinkle gaming elements into our lessons, from badges to leaderboards. Suddenly, my students weren't just studying; they were playing, engaging, and challenging themselves. We dabbled in educational games that demanded strategy, critical thinking, and creativity. I watched in astonishment as they navigated problems with enthusiasm, their faces lit up by the joy of discovery.

Around that time, I began to integrate multimedia into our routine. I'd play a thought-provoking video, throw in an interactive simulation, or even give them a virtual reality headset to explore new dimensions. These tools gave my students a taste of real-world challenges and a playground to test their problem-solving skills.

And finally, we embraced the magic of independent exploration! I nudged my students towards self-reliance, letting them harness the vast internet to feed their curiosities. Armed with resources and search engines, they transformed into little detectives, sifting through data, hunting solutions, and piecing together answers. As they surfed the web, I emphasized the importance of discerning credible from questionable sources.

When I first began teaching, I could never have imagined how technology would completely revamp my students' creative horizons. The digital age has reshaped learning in ways we'd only dreamed of.

I remember the first time one of my students, Jamie, showed me a piece of digital art she'd crafted. She had used a simple tool online, but the result was nothing short of magnificent. It wasn't just the technical skill displayed, but the emotion and depth it conveyed. The layers of textures, the play of light and shadow, and the way she had captured movement within a digital image were captivating. Jamie had seamlessly integrated multimedia elements into her image. She added subtle animations to make parts of her artwork come to life, and embedded soundscapes that enhanced the viewing experience. Gentle rustling of leaves, the distant call of birds, and a soft, flowing stream could be heard as you explored her creation, making it an immersive, multisensory experience.

Seeing her work was a moment of revelation. It was clear that the digital tools at her disposal had unlocked a new level of expression for her. She wasn't just creating art; she was building an entire world, rich with stories and emotions, using the technology available to her.

From digital paintings to multimedia presentations, and even crafting their own little corner of the internet with personal websites, my students were no longer confined to paper and pencils. The world was their canvas, and every tool they needed was right at their fingertips. Jamie's masterpiece was a testament to the boundless possibilities that technology can offer in the hands of young, creative minds.

What's more, the walls of our classroom began to expand. Thanks to online platforms, my students connected with peers across the globe, exchanging ideas, critiquing art, and understanding the vast spectrum of human creativity. By opening up to diverse perspectives, they not only honed their creative instincts, but also learned to appreciate the mosaic of ideas that different cultures bring.

One of the most exciting shifts I observed was in their approach to challenges. Traditional problems were replaced with interactive games or real-world simulations, pushing them to think outside the box. I'd often see them huddled in groups, brainstorming solutions, and celebrating every small win. It was evident: technology wasn't just aiding their learning; it was amplifying their problem-solving prowess.

But among all these shifts, what touched me the most was the personal growth each student experienced. Thanks to tech advancements like AI, their learning experiences became tailored, almost bespoke. It felt like every tool and app was whispering, "What ignites your passion?" This personal touch in education has allowed them to dive deep into subjects they love, making learning a journey of discovery rather than a chore.

There has been a vast sea of change in education, with technology operating as the wind in its sails. We've moved from static lessons to dynamic explorations, from mere absorption of knowledge to vibrant creation. And as the narrative of 'Revitalizing Education' unfolds, we face an exciting future: a world where every student finds their unique spark and lights up the world with their creativity.

In this journey, technology wasn't just a prop; it was the stage, the actor, and the script. And as my students shifted from passive consumers to vibrant creators, I felt a profound sense of accomplishment. For in this digital era, they weren't just learning; they were thriving.

Chapter 2:
How Technology Changes How Students Learn

"The function of education is to teach one to think intensively and to think critically. Intelligence plus character - that is the goal of true education."

- Martin Luther King Jr.

At High Tech High in San Diego, California, the integration of technology into project-based learning has led to notable positive outcomes. By utilizing digital tools such as video editing software, 3D printers, and coding platforms, students engage in hands-on projects that demand creativity, critical thinking, and problem-solving skills. As a result of these innovative approaches, the school has observed increased student engagement, higher attendance rates, and improvements in academic performance. Students' grades have risen, reflecting their deeper understanding and mastery of subjects.

Moreover, the school has noted that students are more motivated and invested in their learning, often going beyond the required curriculum to explore additional areas of interest. The technology-driven projects have not only fostered academic growth but also encouraged students to develop essential life skills, such as collaboration and communication, better preparing them for future academic and professional challenges.

Another example is the Khan Academy, an online educational platform offering various interactive lessons and exercises. Khan Academy incorporates technology to provide students with personalized learning experiences that encourage problem-solving and critical thinking. Through interactive exercises and simulations, students can apply their knowledge to real-world scenarios and develop creative solutions. For example, in the math section, students are presented with challenging word problems that require them to think critically and apply problem-solving strategies to find the solution.

Khan Academy has demonstrated its effectiveness in various educational settings through multiple research studies. These studies provide strong evidence supporting the platform's positive impact on student learning outcomes.

One significant study conducted by Ferman, Finamor, and Lima (2019) involved a large-scale randomized-control trial across 157 primary schools in Brazil. The findings revealed that weekly usage of Khan Academy significantly improved math scores and attitudes toward math when implemented with adequate support.[1]

Another study by Buchel et al. (2019), conducted with approximately 3,500 third- to sixth-grade students in El Salvador, found that supplemental use of Khan Academy resulted in better math scores compared to teacher-only interventions. This randomized-control trial emphasized the platform's effectiveness in enhancing students' math performance.[1]

Moreover, a study by Snipes et al. (2015) in a Silicon Valley school district showed that students who used Khan Academy during a 19-day summer program exhibited better algebra readiness scores. This study highlights the platform's potential to prepare students for higher-level math courses.[1]

A literature review published in the Journal of Environmental and Science Education discussed the effectiveness of Khan Academy in supporting science learning during the COVID-19 pandemic. The review indicated that

---

1 "Multiple Studies Show Khan Academy Drives Learning Gains: Evidence for Our Platform's Effectiveness," *Khan Academy Blog*, January 10, 2024, https://blog.khanacademy.org/multiple-studies-show-khan-academy-drives-learning-gains-evidence-for-our-platforms-effectiveness/.

integrating Khan Academy into science lessons helped improve students' mastery of online learning skills, provided effective student progress monitoring, and supported classroom management.[2]

These studies underscore the value of Khan Academy in promoting critical thinking, problem-solving, and academic achievement. The platform's ability to offer personalized, engaging, and interactive learning experiences has made it a valuable tool in modern education.

To illustrate this point, many teachers have successfully integrated technology into their classrooms to inspire creativity and problem-solving skills. One example is the use of digital storytelling tools. Teachers can encourage students to create digital stories using platforms like Adobe Spark or Storybird. By combining text, images, and multimedia elements, students can express their creativity and develop problem-solving skills as they plan and structure their stories. This activity also allows students to think critically about the narrative and engage in peer feedback, further enhancing their problem-solving abilities.

Schools like High Tech High and online platforms like Khan Academy have demonstrated the effectiveness of incorporating technology into education. Additionally, teachers can leverage digital tools such as storytelling platforms to foster creativity and problem-solving in the classroom. By embracing technology as a tool, educators can provide students with engaging learning experiences that promote critical thinking and creativity.

How Technology Changes Student Learning

Technology is revolutionizing the way students think critically. Picture this: with just a few clicks, students dive into a sea of information, exploring various perspectives, analyzing data, and evaluating sources. This matter

---

2   Angelina Amalia Putri, "The Effectiveness of Khan Academy as a Science Learning Support to Improve Student's Mastery of Skills: Literature Review," *Journal of Environmental and Science Education* 1, no. 2 (2021): 52–56, https://doi.org/10.15294/jese.v1i2.50370.

isn't just about gathering information; it's about synthesizing it to form well-informed opinions. It's exciting to see how they're learning to question, analyze, and make decisions based on solid evidence. It's like watching young detectives at work!

Digital tools are transforming education. Imagine educational apps and online platforms as virtual playgrounds where students encounter real-world problems. These aren't just games; they're challenges that require sharp thinking, application of knowledge, and innovative solutions. It's fascinating to see students engage in these activities, flexing their critical thinking muscles.

But there's more. Technology isn't just a solo journey; it's a collaborative adventure. Through online forums, video calls, and shared digital spaces, students engage in vibrant discussions, exchange ideas, and offer feedback. This collaborative atmosphere is a hotbed for critical thinking. Students are learning to embrace different viewpoints, challenge assumptions, and defend their ideas with logic. It's like watching a lively, intellectual jam session.

Let's not forget the virtual worlds of simulations and experiments. In these digital labs, students are like young scientists or engineers, conducting experiments, analyzing results, and drawing conclusions. This hands-on approach isn't just fun; it's a powerful way to nurture critical thinking. They're connecting theory with practice and developing strategies to tackle complex problems.

Think about creativity and problem-solving. With tools like coding platforms, multimedia software, and design programs, students aren't just learning; they're creating. They're solving puzzles, expressing their creativity, and critically assessing the impact of their work. It's a process that hones their ability to analyze, innovate, and solve real-world challenges.

Technology's role in fostering critical thinking is immense. It offers a treasure trove of resources, from information access to creative tools. It's thrilling to watch how students use these resources to sharpen their critical thinking skills, turning them into active and engaged participants in the digital world.

Lastly, let's explore the intersection of tech and creativity. It's a vibrant space where technology meets artistic expression. Digital art programs, for instance, are playgrounds where students experiment and unleash their creativity. And what about personalized learning experiences? They're custom-made educational journeys, allowing students to explore at their own pace and dive deep into their passions. By integrating technology in education, we're not just teaching; we're inspiring the next generation of creative thinkers and problem solvers. Isn't that an exciting prospect? Let's embrace this journey and create a culture of innovation with the amazing tools at our disposal!

Best Practices in Educational Technology

The advent of educational technology has widened the horizons of learning possibilities and has added depth to the educational experience. Yet, as with all tools, the potency of EdTech lies not just in its existence but in its proper utilization. Understanding both the 'what' and the 'how' becomes paramount.

A research study by the US Department of Education found that merely providing students with technology did not necessarily lead to better learning outcomes. What mattered more was how the technology was integrated into the learning process. Just as a scalpel, in the hands of a novice, can do more harm than good, EdTech tools need expertise, understanding, and thoughtful implementation to truly shine.

Effective Use of Technology in Classrooms

Technology should not be integrated into the curriculum just for its own sake. Instead, its use should align with specific learning objectives. Tools and platforms should be chosen based on how they can enhance learning experiences or provide solutions to specific educational challenges.

When introducing a new tool, ensure students understand not just its functionalities but also its purpose in their learning journey. This not only boosts engagement but also aids in effective utilization.

Just because a tool was effective a year ago doesn't mean it's still the best option now. Regularly review and assess the efficacy of the tools you're using. Seek feedback from students and adjust accordingly.

Ethical Use of Technology

With the increasing integration of digital tools, data privacy has emerged as a significant concern. Ensure the tools and platforms chosen adhere to local and international data protection standards. Articles like "Understanding FERPA, CIPA and Other K–12 Student Data Privacy Laws?" from EdTech Magazine delve deep into this concern.[3]

Teach students how to be good digital citizens. Equip students with the knowledge and skills to navigate the digital realm responsibly. Discussions can encompass topics like cyberbullying, recognizing and combatting misinformation, and understanding one's digital footprint. Resources like the article "4 Strategies for Teaching Media Literacy" from Edutopia provide valuable insights.[4]

Technology needs to be accessible. Ensure that all students, regardless of their abilities or backgrounds, have equal access to technology and can utilize it effectively. This is not just an ethical imperative but also a legal one in many jurisdictions.

Educational technology offers a world of opportunities, but with

---

3 Adam Stone, "Understanding FERPA, CIPA and Other K–12 Student Data Privacy Laws," *EdTech Magazine*, April 2022, https://edtechmagazine.com/k12/article/2022/04/understanding-ferpa-cipa-and-other-k-12-student-data-privacy-laws-perfcon.

4 Julia Boudreau, "4 Strategies for Teaching Media Literacy," *Edutopia*, September 28, 2021, https://www.edutopia.org/article/4-strategies-teaching-media-literacy.

it comes a responsibility. By ensuring a thoughtful, ethical, and effective approach to its integration, we can ensure that we're leveraging its strengths while mitigating potential pitfalls to craft a robust, enriching, and inclusive learning environment for all.

Chapter 3
The Pedagogy of Educational Models

When diving into the world of education, particularly with young minds in the elementary phase, the word model might sound overly technical or even intimidating. But at its core, a model is a structured and consistent way of approaching a subject or a problem. Introducing an educational model like iTECH to elementary students is not about making them follow rigid guidelines but rather about providing a roadmap to navigate the vast landscapes of learning, especially in the ever-evolving realm of technology.

Educators are often already familiar with various models that have proven effective in enhancing learning experiences. For example, Bloom's Taxonomy is a widely used model that categorizes educational goals into a hierarchy, from lower-order thinking skills like remembering and understanding to higher-order skills like analyzing, evaluating, and creating. This model helps teachers design activities and assessments that promote critical thinking and deeper understanding.

Another familiar model is the 5E Instructional Model (Engage, Explore, Explain, Elaborate, Evaluate), which is particularly effective in science education. This model encourages active learning and helps students build on their existing knowledge through hands-on activities and reflection. By following the 5E model, educators can create a dynamic and interactive learning environment that fosters inquiry and curiosity.

The benefit of using these models lies in their ability to provide a clear and systematic approach to teaching and learning. They offer a framework that helps educators plan lessons, assess student progress, and adjust instruction to meet diverse needs. Models like Bloom's Taxonomy and the 5E Instructional Model have been validated through research and practice, demonstrating their effectiveness in promoting student engagement and achievement.

Similarly, the iTECH model offers a structured approach to integrating technology into the classroom. By following the phases of Inspire, Try, Expand, Create, and Huddle, educators can guide students through a process of exploration, experimentation, and reflection. This model not only enhances students' technological skills but also promotes creativity, critical thinking, and collaboration.

By leveraging familiar educational models and introducing new ones like iTECH, educators can create a rich and supportive learning environment that prepares students for the challenges of the digital age. These models provide a roadmap for effective teaching, helping students navigate the complexities of learning and develop the skills needed to succeed.

Why Models Matter in Elementary Education

Children are inherently curious, bursting with questions and a zest to explore. However, the world, even the digital world, can be overwhelming. Without structure, this curiosity can lead to confusion or a lack of direction. Here is where an educational model steps in. It provides a scaffold, supporting students as they construct their understanding and skills.

For young learners, consistency and structure play a pivotal role in creating a safe and familiar environment where they feel empowered to take risks, make mistakes, and learn from them. When they know there's a process to follow, it alleviates the anxiety of the unknown. This is the underlying pedagogy of introducing a model like iTECH. The goal of any educational model is to nurture learners to become creators, thinkers, and problem solvers.

In the heart of a bustling tech-forward school, years of teaching had brought me to a pivotal realization. Gone were the days of the strict curriculum that revolved around familiarizing students with basic technology tools. It was an era of unleashing creativity, of leveraging technology as a canvas upon which young minds painted their most colorful creations.

Drawing inspiration from the ever-evolving realm of educational technology, I found myself contemplating B.F. Skinner's Constructivist Theory of Learning from 1987. Despite the theory's age, it echoed profoundly in the corridors of modern education. Skinner emphasized the significance of building upon prior knowledge, which made me wonder: How does this theory apply in an age where students are born not with a silver spoon but a digital device in their hands?

This led me to carefully study today's students. These are the young souls for whom the internet isn't an innovation—it's their playground. Imagine a world where you never experienced the revelation of the internet coming into your life because it was always there. That's the world of students today. They didn't need a rulebook on how to operate a gadget. For them, it was instinctual, almost second nature. Their approach was more exploratory, not merely about learning a tool but about mastering the art of creation through it.

Structured exploration as a method of learning is not unique to technology or education; it's a universal strategy employed across various domains to optimize skill acquisition and understanding. Structured exploration can be used for any skill, such as childhood play, language learning, and gaming.

Childhood Play

Play is a child's way of learning about the world. Play environments like Montessori or Reggio Emilia provide children with structured environments filled with specific materials or activities and allow children to explore within these confines, learning at their own pace and following their interests.

The Montessori method, developed by Dr. Maria Montessori in the early 1900s, is an educational approach that emphasizes child-led learning within a prepared environment. This method is built on the belief that children are naturally curious and capable of initiating learning in a supportive environment. Montessori classrooms are designed to foster independence, self-discipline, and a love for learning.

Language Learning

Structured exploration learning models effectively guide students from foundational knowledge to advanced application through a series of scaffolded steps. This process is evident in many language courses, where students begin with structured grammar lessons and vocabulary acquisition. Initially, students memorize simple vocabulary and sentence structures, which provide the building blocks for more complex language use.

As students gain proficiency, they transition to more interactive and exploratory activities. For example, they may engage in role-plays that simulate real-life conversations, encouraging them to apply their knowledge in practical contexts. These structured activities help students practice and internalize the language in a controlled environment.

As they progress, students are encouraged to participate in free conversations, where they can use the language more spontaneously and creatively. This stage allows them to explore the language more deeply, using it to express their thoughts and ideas in a less constrained manner. Writing short stories or essays is another method that enables students to explore and experiment with the language, enhancing their understanding and fluency.

As their skills develop, students are given opportunities to use the language in real-world settings. This might involve communicating with native speakers, either in person or through digital platforms. Initially, their communication might be basic and rudimentary, but with continued practice, their proficiency grows. They begin to navigate more complex interactions and conversations, eventually reaching a level where they can effectively communicate with anyone who speaks the language.

Gaming

Many modern video games use structured exploration as an effective learning method. Players are often introduced to game mechanics in a structured tutorial, which guides them through the basic controls and actions required to play the game. As they master initial skills, they're given more freedom to explore the game world and devise their own strategies.

Take, for example, learning to play "Sonic the Hedgehog" on a Sega gaming system. It starts with a basic tutorial level, which serves to familiarize players with Sonic's core abilities. In the Green Hill Zone, players learn how to move Sonic left and right, make him jump, and utilize his spin attack. This level is designed to be straightforward, with clear paths and gentle slopes, allowing players to practice these basic moves without facing overwhelming challenges.

As players progress through the Green Hill Zone, they encounter various elements that gradually increase in complexity. For instance, they might come across springs that launch Sonic into the air, loop-de-loops that test their timing, and enemies that require precise jumping or spinning to defeat. These challenges are introduced incrementally, ensuring that players have ample opportunity to master each new skill before moving on.

Once players are comfortable with the basic mechanics, the game opens up to more complex and varied levels. Zones like the Marble Zone and the

Labyrinth Zone present new obstacles and enemies, requiring players to think strategically navigating the environment and utilizing Sonic's abilities. In these stages, players must apply their learned skills to solve puzzles, avoid hazards, and defeat more challenging foes.

By the time players reach later levels, such as the Star Light Zone and Scrap Brain Zone, they have developed a deep understanding of the game's mechanics and are equipped to tackle the most difficult challenges. These advanced levels encourage players to experiment with different strategies and approaches, fostering creativity and problem-solving skills.

This structured exploration model enhances the gaming experience and mirrors effective educational practices. By gradually introducing new concepts and allowing for incremental mastery, players (or students) build confidence and competence. They are then empowered to explore more freely, apply their knowledge in novel ways, and devise their strategies.

The power of structured exploration lies in its ability to balance guidance with freedom. It allows learners to build foundational skills and knowledge while also fostering creativity, autonomy, and a deeper understanding through self-directed exploration.

From this melting pot of observations, insights, and years of hands-on experience, the iTECH model was birthed, a systematic yet flexible approach to teaching technology in the classroom.

Chapter 4
The iTECH model:
A Revolutionary Approach

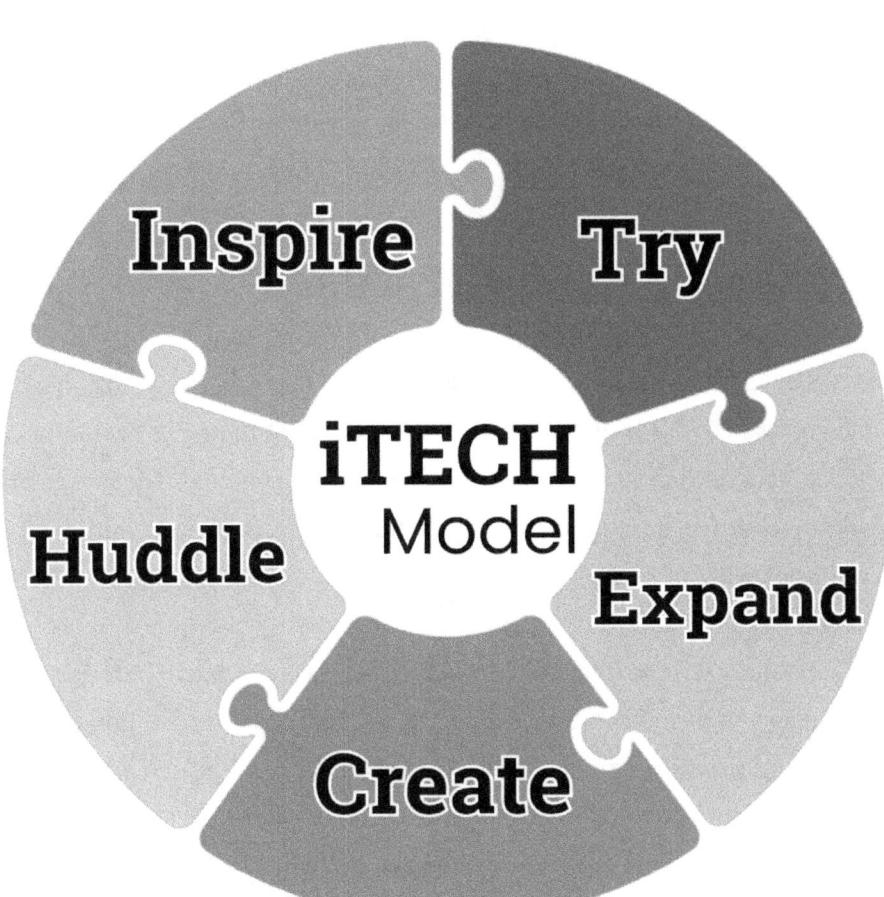

The genius of the iTECH model lies in its balance. It offers the much-needed structure that elementary students crave while also ensuring ample space for exploration, creativity, and autonomy—key ingredients for meaningful learning in the digital age.

As educators, our goal is to not only teach children the 'what,' but also the 'how' and 'why'. The iTECH model is pedagogically sound for elementary students because it mirrors the natural learning process: sparking interest, diving in hands-on, reflecting on discoveries, applying newfound knowledge, and then sharing and receiving feedback.

Remember, at the heart of any educational model is the unwavering goal of nurturing learners who are not only consumers of knowledge but also creators, thinkers, and problem solvers. Let's embark on this journey together to harness the potential of the iTECH model for the learners in our classrooms.

The Skeptic's Transformation

Mrs. Sanders had always prided herself on being a forward-thinking educator. When she heard about the iTECH model during a professional development session, she couldn't help but raise an eyebrow. The presenters made it sound so groundbreaking, yet she had reservations. "Introducing a tech tool without much instruction? Seems like a recipe for chaos," she thought.

The school year started, and Mrs. Sanders was preparing to introduce her students to a new digital storytelling tool. Normally, she'd have PowerPoint slides ready, detailed worksheets on each feature of the tool, and a structured lesson plan. But after hearing her colleague, Mr. Jensen, rave about his experience with the iTECH model, she thought, "Why not give it a try? What's the worst that could happen?"

She meticulously planned the Inspire phase. Rather than her usual approach, she decided to show a 2-minute animated clip made using the story-telling tool. The clip was about a young girl's adventure in a digital world, overcoming obstacles utilizing the tool's features. There was no mention of the tool's name or its specific functionalities—just a captivating story.

As the animation ended, she took a deep breath and looked at her students, expecting a slew of questions about instructions and steps. But to her surprise, the room was alive with excitement.

"That was so cool, Mrs. Sanders! Did the girl really use the app for those effects?"

"Can we make stories like that?"

"I bet I could make an even better adventure!"

The bell hadn't even rung, and her students were already brainstorming story ideas and discussing possible digital effects. Mrs. Sanders was in awe. There was no confusion, just pure, unbridled enthusiasm.

The next day, when she finally introduced the tool and let her students play around with it, their creativity was boundless. They explored the software's features with the same excitement and curiosity they'd shown the previous day. The entire experience was a revelation for Mrs. Sanders. The Inspire phase hadn't created chaos; it had ignited passion.

During a coffee break later that week, she shared her experience with Mr. Jensen. "I couldn't believe it," she said. "The iTECH model, especially that Inspire phase, completely shifted how I think about introducing topics. It's like I've been given a new lens to view teaching."

Mr. Jensen smiled, "It's all about lighting that initial spark. Once that's done, the learning just flows."

From that day on, Mrs. Sanders became a fervent advocate for the iTECH model. She had seen firsthand its power to engage and inspire, turning even the most mundane lessons into captivating journeys of discovery. The Inspire phase had transformed her students' learning experience and rekindled her own passion for teaching.

Components of the iTECH Model

Inspire

The first step was about lighting a spark, not dumping a bucket of information. I remember watching two educators introduce the StopMotion app: one began with instructions, the other with inspiration. The difference was clear. The teacher who inspired students began by showing an exciting short film created using the app, igniting their curiosity and imagination. Students resonate more with a sense of discovery than with a list of directions.

Try

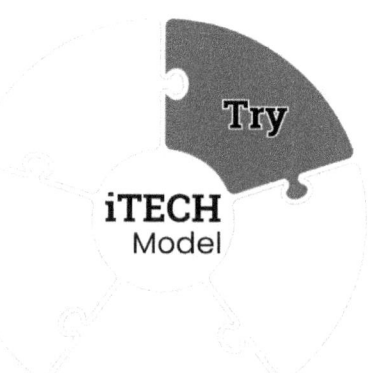

Then, it was time to let the students loose, granting them those golden moments of exploration. It was fascinating, and slightly chaotic, watching them dive into a new tool, discovering its capabilities, sharing their revelations, and occasionally getting wonderfully sidetracked.

Expand

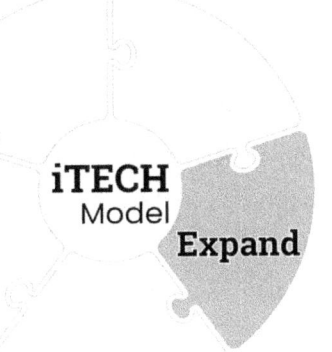

Post-exploration, it was time for a 'Tech Talk.' This was a chance for them to come together, discuss, share, and sometimes even correct misconceptions. As an educator, this was my opportunity to guide, introduce context, and build upon their findings.

Create

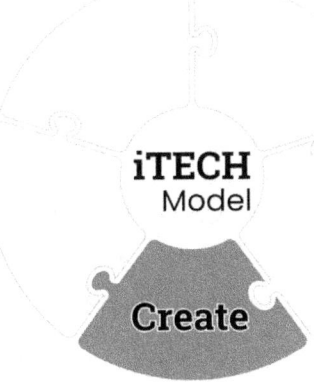

The canvas was set, and the paint was ready. The students were now primed to craft, to mold, to create. Using their newfound knowledge, they began producing content, from educational videos to digital artworks. As their skills expanded, so did their options, with students picking their preferred tools for different projects.

Huddle

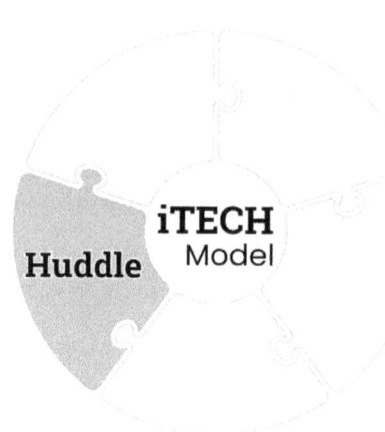

iTECH
Model
Huddle

Finally, the creations needed an audience, a community. Students today don't just see the internet as a space to project their voices; they see it as a space to engage and interact. The 'Huddle' was about sharing, feedback, and collaboration. Tools like Padlet became avenues for students to not only showcase their work but also learn from their peers.

Throughout the evolution of the iTECH model, the journey was as much mine as it was of my students. It redefined teaching, making it less about instructions and more about inspiration. And as classrooms echoed with clicks, swipes, and excited whispers of discovery, I knew education had transformed, and we were ready for the future.

Using a 5-part model, like the iTECH model, to introduce a tech tool to today's students can be exceptionally effective for various reasons:

1. **Tailored for Digital Literacy Building:** Today's students have grown up in an environment saturated with technology. This means they often approach new tech tools not as isolated pieces of software or hardware to master but as components of a broader digital ecosystem they are already familiar with. A multi-step model acknowledges and utilizes this inherent familiarity.

2. **Structured Exploration:** While students today are often comfortable diving into new technologies, a structured approach ensures they explore the tool's essential features. The Try phase in the iTECH model provides a controlled yet explorative environment, promoting

curiosity without overwhelming them.

3. **Building on Prior Knowledge:** Drawing from Skinner's Constructivist Theory, the model emphasizes building on what students already know. Each step of the model gradually layers information, allowing students to connect new insights with prior knowledge and foster deeper understanding.

4. **Promotes Active Learning:** Active learning is a pedagogical approach where students engage with the material, participate in the learning process, and are actively involved in problem-solving. The iTECH model encourages students to be proactive, from trying out the tool independently to creating something with it.

5. **Encourages Collaboration:** The Expand and Huddle stages emphasize sharing and feedback. This not only helps in reinforcing learning but also fosters a sense of community and collaborative learning. Sharing their findings and creations can also boost students' confidence.

6. **Flexibility and Choice:** The Create phase of the model lets students choose how to use the tool, tapping into their intrinsic motivation. As they become more familiar with various tools, they can decide which one best suits their needs for a particular project, promoting autonomy in learning.

7. **Feedback and Reflection:** The model isn't just about using a tool; it's about understanding its strengths, weaknesses, and potential applications. By sharing and receiving feedback during the Huddle phase, students can reflect on their approach, leading to improved future outcomes.

8. **Prepares for Real-world Challenges:** The real world isn't about rote learning; it's about understanding concepts, applying them

innovatively, collaborating, and constantly adapting. The iTECH model mimics these real-world challenges, making students better prepared for future tech encounters.

9. **Teacher as a Facilitator:** Instead of being the sole source of knowledge, the teacher acts as a guide or facilitator in this model, allowing students to take charge of their learning. This can be more engaging for students and aligns with modern pedagogical shifts.

10. **Relevance:** Technology is not static. It's continually evolving, and so is the way we interact with it. A multi-part model ensures that teaching methods remain relevant, adapting to both the technological landscape and the evolving dynamics of student engagement.

Inclusivity & Accessibility

The iTECH model's success doesn't just rest on how innovative or engaging the tools are but on how inclusive and universally designed they are to cater to every student's unique needs.

Technology Adaptations for Diverse Needs

1. **Assistive Technology:** Analyze the integration of tools tailored for students with disabilities. This includes text-to-speech functions, screen readers, or adaptive keyboards that assist in ensuring these students can access and engage with the content just as effectively as their peers.

2. **Language Tools:** For ELL students, the inclusion of translation tools, multi-language dictionaries, or language learning apps can make a

world of difference. Monitor how frequently and effectively these are integrated into lessons.

Socio-economic Considerations

1. **Affordable Tech Solutions:** Not all students have access to high-end gadgets. Ensure that the digital tools and platforms suggested in the iTECH model are affordable or offer free versions that do not compromise the learning experience.

2. **Internet Accessibility:** Recognize that not all students have high-speed internet at home. The iTECH model can thus also integrate offline functionalities, or schools might consider initiatives like providing mobile hotspots to ensure uninterrupted learning.

Universal Design for Learning (UDL)

1. **Multiple Means of Representation:** The content can be presented in diverse ways to cater to different learning styles. For instance, a historical event can be taught through a video, a podcast, an interactive timeline, or a digital comic.

2. **Multiple Means of Action & Expression:** Students should have varied avenues to express their understanding, be it through digital art, online quizzes, interactive presentations, or collaborative projects.

3. **Multiple Means of Engagement:** Tap into students' interests and challenges by offering choices. For instance, while learning about ecosystems, some might prefer a virtual reality forest exploration, while others might opt for a data-driven simulation game.

Feedback and Continuous Adaptation

1. **Regular Check-ins:** Through feedback forms or individual discussions, regularly check with students and educators about any accessibility or inclusivity issues they might face. This ensures that any challenges are promptly addressed.

2. **Professional Development:** Teachers should be trained in using technology inclusively. Workshops on UDL, assistive technology, or ELL strategies can be immensely beneficial.

In the grand tapestry of the modern classroom, each student brings a unique shade, a distinct pattern. The success of the iTECH model is, in part, determined by how vividly and fairly each of these patterns is allowed to shine. In championing inclusivity and accessibility, we don't just make education fair; we make it richer, more colorful, and immeasurably more profound.

The iTECH Revolution

Dive into the world of the iTECH teaching model, and you'll be astounded by the transformation it ushers into your classroom. Not only will you rekindle your passion for incorporating technology into your lessons, but you'll also witness an elevated level of engagement, curiosity, and creativity from your students. These changes are not just a hypothesis; they are tangible and transformative outcomes. By embracing this model, you'll be equipping your students with skills and competencies that will prove invaluable in the modern world.

When you witness these positive changes, don't keep them to yourself. Let your experiences resonate beyond the confines of your classroom walls. Engage your administrators and colleagues, allowing them to see the power and potential of the iTECH model. Encourage them to become familiar with the International Society for Technology in Education (ISTE) standards, emphasizing the significance of the Innovative Designer, Computational Thinker, and Global Collaborator standards. These are not just mere labels; they represent the evolution of teaching and learning, placing you at the vanguard of this educational revolution.

The confidence with which I endorse this model is not born from mere theory or a fleeting trend in education. Over a span of six months, I spearheaded a comprehensive research study, closely collaborating with both technology educators and classroom teachers at the elementary level. The findings were nothing short of remarkable. As teachers reshaped their instructional methodologies, leveraging the iTECH model's strengths, they witnessed students rising to the occasion, showing unparalleled enthusiasm and competency. The model's efficacy was clear.

So, step forward with conviction, knowing that the iTECH model isn't just another pedagogical tool; it's a catalyst for change. Embrace it, adapt it, and witness the growth of your students and the rejuvenation of your teaching methods. The future of education beckons, and you, dear educator, are poised to lead the way.

Chapter 5
Cross-Curricular Benefits

The strength of the iTECH model doesn't lie merely in introducing students to technology but in the universal skills it nurtures. Each phase of the model inherently promotes competencies that are critical across all subjects. Let's delve deeper into how the model encourages the development of skills like critical thinking, creativity, collaboration, and communication (often referred to as the "4 Cs" of 21st-century education).

For instance, a teacher might begin the journey by showing students an innovative project created using a particular tech tool, sparking their curiosity and encouraging them to think critically about how it was made.

Critical Thinking

The *Try* and *Expand* phases of the model challenge students to independently explore and then critically discuss the digital tools at their disposal. As they navigate unfamiliar interfaces, make choices on their usage, and dispel myths about the tool, they are constantly engaging in analysis, evaluation, and decision-making. For example, a science class might involve students hypothesizing the outcome of a virtual experiment. As they navigate the tool, make decisions, and evaluate results, they exercise their critical thinking skills, much like analyzing a character's motives in a literature class or interpreting data in social studies.

Creativity

The *Create* phase stands out as a testament to the model's commitment to fostering creativity. Giving students the agency to produce something original using the digital tools they've explored encourages them to think outside of the box. For instance, in a math class, students might use graphing software to create visual representations of complex equations. Or, in an art class, they could design digital artwork, stretching their imagination and creative thinking.

Collaboration

Throughout the iTECH model, there's a strong emphasis on collaborative learning, especially evident in the *Huddle* phase. Sharing creations and seeking feedback is a group activity, mirroring real-world scenarios where teamwork is pivotal. Similarly, in subjects like history or literature, group discussions or collaborative projects can provide diverse perspectives, enriching the overall understanding of a topic.

Communication

The *Expand* and *Huddle* phases, which involve "Tech Talks" and feedback sessions, inherently foster effective communication skills. Whether it's articulating their discoveries or offering constructive critiques, students learn the art of clear and effective communication. This skill is invaluable, be it presenting a scientific hypothesis, debating a point in civics, or narrating a story in language arts.

In essence, the iTECH model isn't just about integrating technology; it's about molding students to be well-rounded individuals, ready to tackle challenges across subjects. Its universal approach ensures that the skills they pick up are not just applicable to a technology lesson but are also transferable and valuable across the curriculum.

Chapter 6

A Day in the Life of Ms. Ramirez: Harnessing the Power of a Tech-Rich Environment

When Ms. Ramirez started teaching at Parkside Elementary five years ago, the school was taking its first baby steps into integrating technology. But over the years, thanks to visionary administration and collaborative staff, Parkside transformed into a tech haven with the iTECH model at its heart.

Every morning, Ms. Ramirez's students walk into a colorful, dynamic classroom where technology isn't just a tool—it's an extension of their learning experience. The room is equipped with interactive smartboards, a tech corner with tablets and laptops, and a makerspace with 3D printers and robotics kits. The air buzzes with palpable excitement.

One of Ms. Ramirez's favorite implementations of the iTECH model is her monthly "Innovation Day." Here's how it goes:

Inspire Phase: To kick off the lesson, Ms. Ramirez begins with a compelling video of a marine biologist exploring the Great Barrier Reef. The vibrant underwater scenes, accompanied by the biologist's enthusiastic narration, captivate the students. She can see their eyes light up as the video showcases the diversity of marine life and the beauty of coral reefs. After the video ends, she doesn't dive into the details of the digital poster app just yet. Instead, she asks the students what inspired them most about the video.

Students excitedly respond:

- "I loved the colorful fish and the way they swim through the coral!"

- "The biologist said the reefs are like underwater cities. That's so cool!"

- "I didn't know that coral reefs are home to so many different animals!"

Try Phase: With the students buzzing with inspiration, Ms. Ramirez introduces the Digital Poster app. She encourages them to explore the app independently or in pairs, focusing on creating posters related to marine conservation. She provides minimal guidance, allowing them to discover the app's features on their own.

As students navigate the app, they experiment with various tools and options:

- "Check out this cool background I found! It looks like the ocean floor."

- "I can add text here about why coral reefs are important."

- "Look, I found a way to include a video clip of the reef!"

Ms. Ramirez observes their interactions, noting how they manipulate images, adjust text, and experiment with layout designs. She sees them learning through exploration and figuring out how to convey their messages effectively through the app.

Expand Phase: After the exploration period, Ms. Ramirez gathers the students for a "Tech Talk." She invites them to share their discoveries and tips with the class. The students are eager to showcase what they've learned and help each other out.

The discussion is lively:

- "I figured out how to change the font size and color to make the text stand out more."

- "You can add animations to your poster! It makes the fish look like they're swimming."

- "There's a feature where you can add sound clips. I added ocean sounds to my poster."

Ms. Ramirez takes the opportunity to dispel any misconceptions and highlight key features of the app. She emphasizes the importance of clear messaging in their posters and suggests ways to enhance their designs. The students jot down notes and exchange ideas, further refining their skills and understanding of the app.

Create Phase: Armed with inspiration and newfound knowledge, the students dive into creating their digital posters. Ms. Ramirez provides guidelines but encourages creativity and individual expression. Each student selects a specific aspect of marine conservation to focus on, such as the impact of plastic pollution, the importance of coral reefs, or the role of marine protected areas.

The classroom buzzes with activity as students design their posters:

One student creates a vibrant poster with colorful images of marine life and bold text highlighting the dangers of plastic pollution.

Another designs an interactive poster that includes a QR code linking to a video about coral restoration efforts.

A pair of students collaborate on a poster that combines infographics, text, and animated elements to explain the effects of overfishing.

Ms. Ramirez moves around the room, offering feedback and encouragement. She is amazed by the students' creativity and the depth of their understanding. They use the app's features to their fullest potential, creating compelling and informative posters.

Huddle Phase: Once the posters are completed, Ms. Ramirez organizes a "show and tell" session. Students take turns presenting their posters on the smartboard, explaining their design choices and the message they aim to convey. Their peers provide constructive feedback, stating what they like, asking questions, and suggesting improvements.

Some feedback includes:

- "I love how you used animations to show the sea turtle's journey. Maybe you could add a voiceover explaining each stage?"

- "Your infographic is really informative! Have you thought about adding more statistics to support your points?"

- "The augmented reality feature is so cool! Could you add more interactive elements to make it even more engaging?"

Ms. Ramirez also uses the school's Padlet board to pin the students' projects, allowing them to receive feedback from other grades. This not only provides a wider audience but also fosters a sense of community and shared learning.

Reflection: Reflecting on the entire process, Ms. Ramirez feels a sense of accomplishment and growth. She realizes that each phase of the iTECH model has its unique benefits. Seeing her students' engagement and creativity flourish reaffirms her belief in the power of technology-enhanced learning. With each attempt, her confidence grows, and she becomes more adept at guiding her students through the iTECH model, turning each lesson into an inspiring journey of discovery and innovation.

But what truly warms Ms. Ramirez's heart is the tangible growth she observes. Aiden, a quiet boy with a learning disability, often felt overwhelmed with traditional learning methods. But the iTECH model opened up his world. The hands-on, exploratory nature of the approach appealed to his strengths. Over the year, Aiden's animated marine project, infused with his unique creativity and showcasing advanced problem-solving, became one of the class highlights.

The school's tech-rich environment, complemented by the unwavering support of the administration, has given Ms. Ramirez the freedom to experiment and innovate. Professional development workshops keep her updated, while the school's tech support ensures she never faces any tech-related glitches. This has allowed her to shift her role from a traditional instructor to a facilitator of collaborative learning.

Parkside's transformation is evident not just in the state-of-the-art tools, and the iTECH model's smooth integration, but in the gleam of excitement in students' eyes, their heightened creativity, and their evolved problem-solving abilities. For Ms. Ramirez, every day is a testament to the boundless possibilities that a supportive, tech-rich environment can unleash.

Section 2
Phases of the iTECH Model

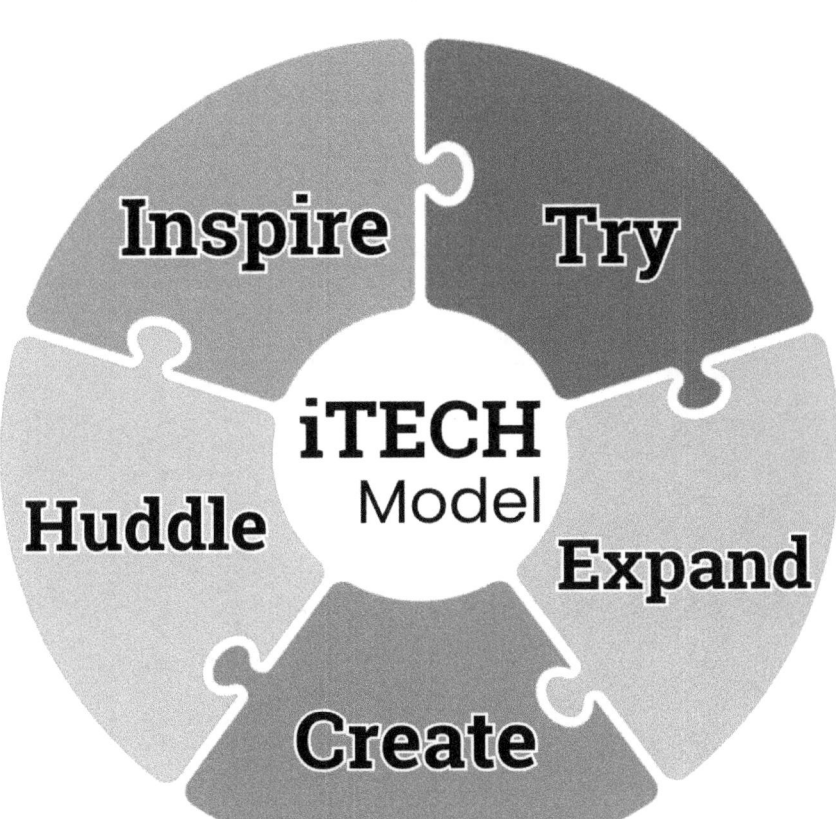

Chapter 7
I for Inspire

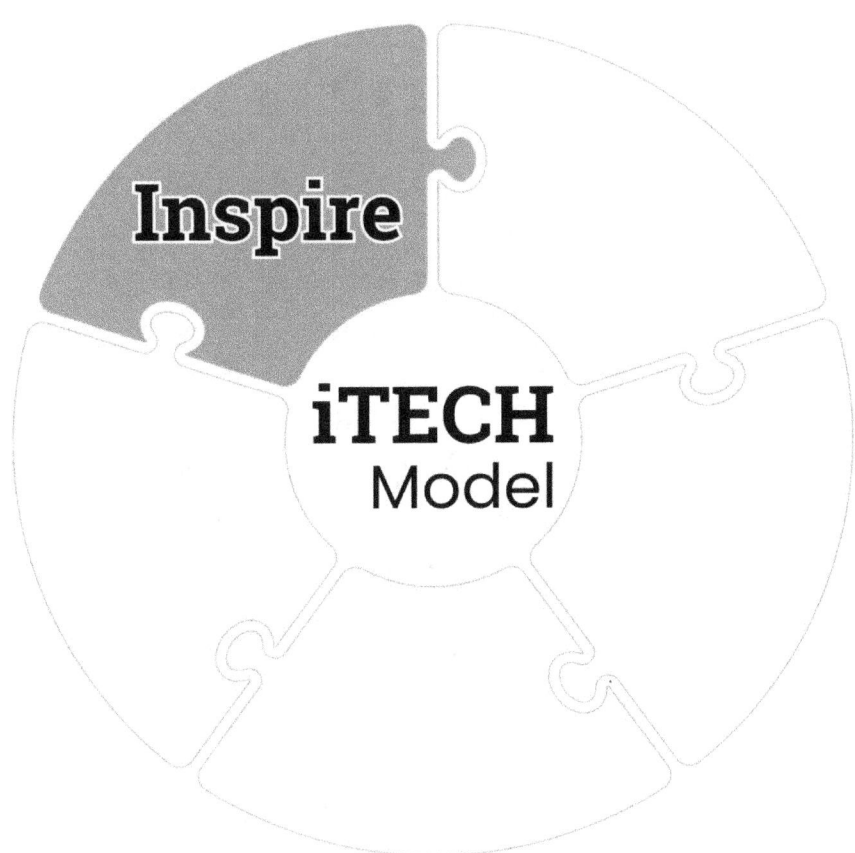

Before any lesson on technology commences, it's pivotal to stir the interest of the students, ignite their curiosity, and ensure they're eager to learn. The Inspire phase is crucial to capture their attention and prepare them for a journey of discovery. The objective is to kickstart students' curiosity and set the stage for exploration without directly diving into the instructional 'how-tos' of a technology tool.

Traditional introductions might front-load information or instructions. In the Inspire phase, the aim is to evoke wonder and inquiry, teasing the potential of what's to come without giving away specifics.

Key Components of the Inspire Phase

To start your lesson with a bang, initiate a quick introductory activity that lasts no more than five minutes. The primary aim of this brief exercise is to grab students' attention and set a dynamic tone for the lesson. Utilize a visual timer to create a sense of anticipation and to help maintain the schedule. Should students become highly engaged, channel their energy towards the Try phase while assuring them their questions will be addressed as the lesson progresses.

During this teacher-directed phase, it's important to note that, while the primary goal is to spark interest, you control the direction and pacing of the activity. Students do not need any prior knowledge about the tool or the topic to participate fully, making it accessible for everyone. Subtly guide students on what to focus on when they begin their exploration. This should be more of a gentle nudge rather than a detailed step-by-step instruction. This approach helps maintain the element of discovery and engagement as they move forward in the lesson.

Over my years of teaching, I've found that the best content elicits a "wow" factor. Consider what element of the tech tool might fascinate your students the most and lead with that. It's often a blend of the tool's potential and its relevance to the learners' world.

Think of the Inspire phase as a movie trailer. You want to give away enough to intrigue but not so much that the entire plot is revealed. Keep them guessing!

To assess the effectiveness of the Inspire phase, look for signs of curiosity, such as questions they're asking, discussions they're having, or even that gleam in their eyes. Active engagement is a positive sign. A classroom buzzing with excitement, students leaning in, or hands shooting up with questions are all good indicators.

For resources for the Inspire phase, digital media, like short, engaging videos or GIFs related to the tech tool, can be wonders. Even student-created content from previous years can be showcased. Multimedia can be particularly effective in grabbing attention, and it is very much encouraged.

To transition from the Inspire phase to the Try phase, I often pose a guiding question or challenge, leading students into exploration. For instance, "Now that we've seen what's possible, how might you use this tool to create something amazing?"

Challenges of the Inspire Phase

When students are uninspired, it's crucial to gauge their hesitation. Is it fear of tech, a lack of understanding, or something else? Addressing this can often turn the tide.

If you notice diminishing returns or if there are new features in a tech tool, then it's time to tweak or overhaul your Inspire activity.

A frequent pitfall during the Inspire phase is overloading information. Remember, the Inspire phase isn't about instruction; it's about evoking curiosity.

Open dialogue is the key to addressing misconceptions. If students have misconceptions, addressing them in the moment ensures they move forward with clarity.

The technological landscape is ever-evolving, as are our students. It's crucial to stay updated, experiment with new strategies, and adapt based on feedback and results.

The iTECH model is designed to be adaptive and responsive, ensuring our students remain at the center of the learning experience. Your intuition as an educator, combined with these guidelines, will ensure the Inspire phase is consistently impactful.

Inspire in Action: Scenarios to Consider

Scenario A:

Ms. Thompson stood at the front of the classroom as she addressed her fourth-grade students. "All right, class, today we're going to start a new project. We're going to make stop-motion animations," she announced. She clicked to the first slide of her PowerPoint presentation, which displayed a plain text outline of the project steps.

"First, you'll need to come up with a story. Then, you'll create a storyboard. After that, you'll take a series of pictures using the app. Finally, you'll put the pictures together to create an animation," she explained, not bothering to look up from her notes.

Several students exchanged puzzled glances, clearly unsure of what stop-motion animation was. Ms. Thompson didn't seem to notice their confusion. "I'll hand out the worksheets now. They list all the steps you need to follow," she said, passing out the papers with little enthusiasm.

A hand shot up in the back of the room. "Ms. Thompson, what kind of stories can we make?" asked Sarah, a usually enthusiastic student.

Ms. Thompson shrugged. "It doesn't matter. Just make something up. It can be anything as long as you follow the steps."

Scenario B:

Ms. Anderson gathered her third graders around the smartboard. "Today, we're going to dive into something really exciting!" she announced with a gleam in her eye. The students, sensing the excitement, leaned in, their curiosity piqued.

Ms. Anderson played a short, captivating stop-motion animation video titled "The Adventures of a Tiny Toy." The video depicted a small toy soldier embarking on a grand adventure across a desk, using everyday items as props. The room was filled with gasps and giggles as the students watched the toy soldier come to life.

When the video ended, Ms. Anderson asked, "What did you think? Pretty cool, right?"

"That was awesome! How did they make the toy move like that?" asked Liam, his eyes wide with wonder.

"We're going to figure that out today," Ms. Anderson replied. "By the end of this week, you'll be creating your very own stop-motion animations!"

Which approach sounds more inviting? Which scenario is likely to cultivate a classroom full of eager and motivated tech-intuitive learners? Ideally, Scenario B is more in line with the essence of the Inspire phase. This approach empowers students to lead their exploration while kindling their curiosity about what lies ahead.

Remember that our tech-intuitive learners often don't need detailed instructions right from the start; they thrive on exploration and discovery. While it might be tempting to provide direct instructions, resist the urge to teach the technology tool during the Inspire phase. If the tool you're introducing has multifaceted functionalities, gently guide the students' exploration toward the aspect they will be utilizing for the day's objective. This approach maintains the element of discovery and allows students to engage more deeply with the learning process.

Here are some ways to engage students during the Inspire phase:

1. **Word Clouds:** Mystery Topic Unraveling

   - Begin by showcasing a word cloud with various terms from a topic they've recently studied or will be studying.

   - Ask students to guess the topic or theme based on the words in the cloud.

   - Share that they'll be creating their own word clouds and challenge them to make their peers guess their chosen topics.

2. **Infographics:** Fact Shock Session

   - Display an intriguing infographic with surprising stats or facts. For example, facts about the universe, the human body, or historical events.

   - After discussing the facts, reveal that students will have the chance to create their own infographics about a topic of their choice.

3. **Animations:** Short Animated Story Viewing

   - Show a short, gripping animation clip without dialogue.

   - Have a brief discussion about the storyline, characters, and the emotions conveyed.

   - Announce that they'll be diving into the world of animation and creating their mini-animated stories.

4. **Comic Strips:** Superhero Introduction

   - Begin with a comic strip featuring a new superhero.

   - Discuss their powers, origin story, and challenges.

   - Let students know that they'll have the opportunity to create a comic strip introducing their own superhero or narrating a day in their lives.

5. **Crossword Puzzles:** Classroom Challenge

- Distribute a fun crossword puzzle related to a recent lesson or popular culture.

- After some attempt time, discuss the answers.

- Inform them they'll be crafting their own crossword puzzles. They could create one for a book they've read, a historical event, or even about their classroom community!

6. **Posters:** Mystery Event Teaser

- Display a vibrant poster hinting at an upcoming school event or fictional event without giving away explicit details.

- Engage in a discussion about predicting the event based on the clues from the poster.

- Share that they'll be designing their own posters to promote an event, cause, or project.

In each approach, the key is to initially engage students with an element of surprise, curiosity, or challenge, followed by the revelation that they'll be taking the creative reins in using the respective tech tool. This not only piques their interest but also empowers them with a sense of ownership and anticipation.

Remember, the essence of the Inspire phase is to spark curiosity. Rather than diving straight into instruction, we aim to stimulate student interest, setting the stage for deeper engagement with the technology tool at hand.

Chapter 8
T for Try

Try

iTECH
Model

The Try phase is about giving students a few minutes of freedom to dive into the digital tool. This isn't about mastery or following a prescribed set of tasks; it's about initial interaction, discovery, and sparking interest. The environment is abuzz with enthusiasm, with exclamations of discovery echoing through the room.

The objective is to provide students with an opportunity for independent exploration of a digital tool, fostering curiosity and a sense of discovery without the confines of structured instruction.

Key Components of the Try Phase

The key components of the Try phase are essential for setting the stage for student exploration and discovery. This phase is intentionally brief, lasting only 3-5 minutes. Students can work individually, in pairs, or in small groups. It's important to anticipate and be comfortable with the lively chatter and exclamations as students uncover the tool's features. During this time, the teacher's role is to observe without intervening, providing a golden opportunity to take anecdotal notes and listen to students' interactions, noting any misconceptions or areas of challenge. Students are tasked with accessing the app, website, or program, and exploring its functionalities without specific direction, while pondering how they might create or produce using the tool. Once the timer rings, the Try phase concludes, transitioning students to the Expand phase.

During the Try phase, it's essential to resist the urge to correct or guide students. This time is for the students to feel the tool out independently and make their own discoveries. It's perfectly okay for students to make mistakes during this phase, as this is a crucial part of the learning process. Additionally, taking anecdotal notes during this phase can provide valuable insights for later instructional stages, helping to tailor future guidance and support based on the observations made.

During the Try phase, focus on noting students' interactions, their initial reactions to the tool, any common challenges they face, and particularly innovative or unique ways they use the tool. These observations will inform your instruction in the following phases and provide insights into individual student needs and preferences. This reflective practice ensures that the learning experience is tailored and responsive to student engagement and discovery.

Challenges of the Try Phase

A few common challenges during the Try phase include students becoming frustrated if they can't figure out how the tool works, students requesting help when the goal is for them to try the tool on their own, managing the noise level, and students saying that they are done exploring the tool before the time is up.

Some students may naturally feel a bit of frustration when first introduced to a new tool. The objective of the Try phase is exploration, not mastery. Reassure students that this phase is about discovery and that it's okay not to understand everything immediately. Remind them that the subsequent phases of the iTECH model will provide clarity and guidance, helping them to overcome any initial difficulties.

While the primary goal of the Try phase is for students to explore independently, it's important to gauge the nature of their requests when a student asks for help. If a student has a technical issue accessing the tool, it's appropriate to assist. However, if they're seeking guidance on using the tool, gently remind them that this time is for independent exploration and that detailed guidance will come soon. This approach helps maintain the integrity of the exploration phase.

The Try phase is expected to be lively and buzzing with excitement. Set clear expectations about volume levels before starting, and use classroom signals to remind students to check their volume if it gets too high. Embrace the noise to some extent—it signifies engaged learners actively participating in the learning process.

If some students feel confident with the tool, encourage them to dig deeper by looking for features they might have missed or brainstorming how they might use the tool for a project or assignment. Keeping their engagement levels high is crucial, even if they believe they are done. Encourage continuous exploration and creativity.

Let's look at Ms. Anderson's classroom. Ms. Anderson handed out tablets, each preloaded with a simple digital storytelling app designed for stop-motion animation. "For the next few minutes, I want you to explore this app on your own. Try to figure out how to make a short animation. Remember, there's no right or wrong way to do this—just explore and see what you can discover."

The room buzzed with activity as students began experimenting with the app. Some students worked individually, while others paired up to share ideas.

"Look, I made the toy car move across the screen!" exclaimed Emma, showing her animation to her friend.

"I can't get mine to work," sighed Aiden, tapping the screen in frustration.

"That's okay, Aiden," Ms. Anderson reassured him as she walked by, making a mental note of his struggle. "Remember, this is just our first try. You'll get the hang of it."

Try In Action: Scenarios to Consider

Scenario A:

"Okay, class, now that everyone has their device, we are going to use the StopMotion app to make a video, which you will turn in for a grade. Please tap to open it and follow the seven steps on your worksheet for using the app correctly to make your video."

Scenario B:

"Okay, class, today we are going to use a new digital tool to make a video, which you will be publishing online next week. It is called StopMotion, and it does a lot of cool things. I would like you to take the next 4 minutes to try out the app and see what you can figure out about making a video with it. I put the timer on the board, and the app icon looks like this…Go!"

Which scenario is more likely to give students the opportunity to explore the tool on their own? The Try phase of the iTECH model serves as a reminder that often, the most authentic learning stems from unguided exploration. By allowing students these moments of self-led discovery, they not only become familiar with the tool but also ignite their curiosity and drive to learn more. This sets the stage perfectly for more structured learning in subsequent phases.

Chapter 9
E for Expand

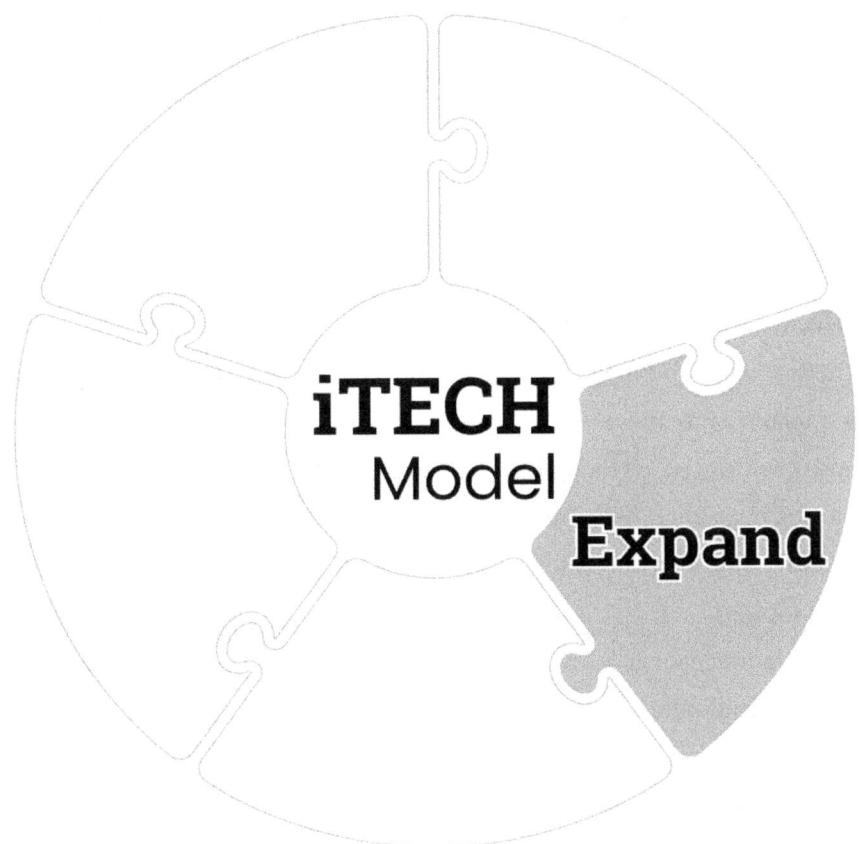

During the Expand phase, students are given the opportunity to share their discoveries, either in pairs or as a whole group. The teacher plays a crucial role in this phase by actively listening to the students, noting their discoveries, and addressing misconceptions. Additionally, the teacher high-lights the crucial features of the digital tool that students need to focus on. New technical terms and icons are introduced during this phase, ideally added to a word wall or an iTECH journal for future reference. This phase also involves clarifying the context for the upcoming task and presenting any design constraints that may be relevant to the students' work.

The objective of the Expand phase is to facilitate a structured discussion where students can share their discoveries from the Try phase. This discussion allows the teacher to address any misconceptions and emphasize essential features of the digital tool, ensuring that students are well-prepared for the subsequent phases of the iTECH model.

Key Components of the Expand Phase

A "Tech Talk" is an integral part of the Expand phase. It is a structured discussion session where students share their findings from the Try phase. For students, this means discussing what they have discovered, what they found exciting or challenging, and any questions they might have. For the teacher, a Tech Talk involves listening attentively, noting key points, correcting any misconceptions, and emphasizing the crucial features of the digital tool.

While the teacher takes a backseat in the Try phase, they play an active role here, guiding discussions, and ensuring accurate understanding. In this stage, the teacher encourages students to openly share their discoveries, building confidence and promoting active participation.

Utilizing the principle that academic discourse enhances retention, ensures that a substantial portion of the session is dedicated to discussion. As students mention new features or functions, the teacher introduces and explains relevant terminology. While students are already thinking about the tool's capabilities, the teacher provides context for how it will be used in the next phase.

When leading the tech talk, listen keenly to understand students' experiences and identify any gaps in their understanding. Ensure all voices are heard. Even if a student's discovery is mentioned by others, it's crucial for their confidence to share. Be prepared by having resources ready, like a digital or physical word wall, to quickly add new terms and icons.

Challenges of the Expand Phase

During the Expand phase of the iTECH model, teachers might face several challenges that require strategic approaches to ensure the phase is effective and inclusive for all students.

One challenge is ensuring that every student has a chance to share during the "Tech Talk," particularly in larger classes. To address this, teachers can have students first share their discoveries in pairs or small groups. After a few minutes, each group can then share one key insight with the whole class. This approach ensures that all students have an opportunity to discuss their findings while still allowing for a variety of insights to be shared within the limited time available.

Another challenge arises when no student has discovered a feature or aspect of the tool that is crucial for the upcoming task. The Expand phase's flexibility allows teachers to introduce any essential features that may have been missed. After students have shared their discoveries, the teacher can highlight the missed feature by saying, "All these features you've discovered are fantastic! There's another helpful tool I'd like you to know about," and then proceed to introduce the necessary feature.

Handling incorrect information or misconceptions without discouraging the student who shared them is another potential challenge. Teachers can approach this with a positive, growth mindset. They might say, "That's an interesting observation, [Student's Name]. It's common to think that way, but actually, here's how it works..." This way, the misconception is corrected in a manner that doesn't make the student feel they made a mistake, thus maintaining their confidence and encouraging further participation.

There might be instances where a teacher is not familiar with all the features of a tool, and a student brings up something new. It's perfectly fine for teachers to not have all the answers. This can be turned into a learning opportunity by saying, "That's a feature I'm not fully familiar with. Can you show us how you used it?" or "Let's explore that together!" This response not only values the students discovery, but also fosters a collaborative learning environment.

Lastly, integrating the "Tech Talk" phase within the constraints of limited lesson time can be challenging. Teachers can shorten the sharing time by implementing a rapid-fire round where students share their findings in keywords or phrases instead of detailed explanations. Alternatively, they could assign a "tech reporter" for the day – one student who summarizes the class's findings concisely. These approaches help ensure that the "Tech Talk" phase is still conducted, even when time is tight.

By anticipating these challenges and applying these strategies, teachers can effectively manage the Expand phase, ensuring it remains a valuable and engaging part of the iTECH model.

Expand in Action:
Scenario from Ms. Anderson

"Alright, class, now that we've had some time to explore the digital story-telling tool and play around with creating stop-motion animations, let's come together for a Tech Talk. This is a time for us to share what we've discovered, ask questions, and learn from each other. Everyone did such a great job during the Try phase, so I'm excited to hear what you've found!

"Who would like to start by sharing something interesting they discovered while working with the tool? It could be a feature you found, something that surprised you, or even something you found challenging."

Aiden answered, "I found out that you can change the background of each frame to make it look like the characters are moving to different places!"

"That's a great discovery!" Ms. Anderson replied. "Changing backgrounds can really make your story more dynamic and interesting. Did anyone else find a similar feature or use backgrounds in their animation?"

"I did!" Michael piped up with excitement. "I used different backgrounds to show my character traveling through a forest and then into a city."

Ms. Anderson transitioned to the next step, addressing challenges. "Now, let's talk about any challenges or things that were confusing. Did anyone come across something they weren't sure how to use?"

"I had trouble figuring out how to make the characters move smoothly. They kept jumping from place to place," Emma answered.

"That's a common challenge with stop-motion animation. One trick is to make very small movements between each frame. This creates the illusion of smooth movement. Did anyone else find a solution to this?"

"I realized that if I moved the character just a tiny bit each time, it looked a lot better," Ben replied.

"Let's talk about some important features we should all be familiar with. One key feature is the frame rate—how many frames per second your animation will play. Did anyone adjust their frame rate?"

"I tried changing the frame rate, but I wasn't sure what was best," Lucas said.

"Good observation. The frame rate can really affect how smooth your animation looks. Usually, a higher frame rate makes the animation smoother, but it also means you need more frames. For most of our projects, around 12-15 frames per second is a good balance. Let's all try adjusting our frame rate during our next project and see what difference it makes.

"Now, let's talk about our upcoming project. We're going to create a short story using our stop-motion animations. Remember, your story should have a clear beginning, middle, and end. You'll also need to use at least three different backgrounds and include some form of dialogue or narration.

"Can anyone tell me why it's important to have a clear structure in your story?"

"So that it's easy to understand and interesting to watch," Dave said.

"Exactly! A clear structure helps keep your audience engaged and makes your story more enjoyable. Also, when you add dialogue or narration, it helps bring your characters to life. Any questions about what we'll be working on?"

The class was silent, clearly understanding their next steps. Ms. Anderson continued, "Great job, everyone! I'm really impressed with all your discoveries and the way you're helping each other out. Remember, the Tech Talk is a time to share and learn together, and you all did fantastic. Now, let's get started on creating our stories! If you have any more questions or need help, feel free to ask."

The Expand phase is the bridging segment between raw exploration and structured understanding. It's where the teacher steps in to guide students, ensuring they have a correct and comprehensive grasp of the digital tool. Through structured "Tech Talk," students not only understand the tool better but also build confidence in their ability to discover and share.

Chapter 10:
C for Create

The Create phase is where the foundational knowledge and exploration coalesce into a tangible product. After familiarizing themselves with the tool and understanding the task's requirements, students engage deeply with their creativity and understanding of the subject to produce an outcome that mirrors their unique perspectives and skills.

The objective is to empower students to harness digital tools in crafting meaningful end products, showcasing their comprehension and creativity while following a given set of design constraints.

In the Create phase, students embark on their creative journey by first understanding the design constraints laid out in the rubric and any other specific guidelines provided by the teacher. This ensures they are clear on what is expected and the boundaries within which they can operate. Having explored the digital tool's functionalities in previous phases, students now apply their understanding to produce the desired outcome. If they are working in groups, effective collaboration and individual contributions from each member are crucial for success. Beyond creating the end product, students can also reflect on their learning process, considering the challenges they faced and how they overcame them.

Key Components of the Create Phase

Promoting creativity is essential during this phase. While students should adhere to the rubric, they should also be encouraged to interpret and present information creatively. The teacher's role is to facilitate rather than dominate, allowing students to take charge of their creations and offering guidance only when necessary or if students veer off track. Celebrate the diversity of creations, especially if students have learned multiple tools and their end products differ widely. Valuing the process over the final product emphasizes the skills acquired and the learning journey, ensuring students gain a deeper understanding and appreciation for their work.

Challenges of the Create Phase

Teachers might face several challenges during the Create phase of the iTECH model. One common issue is determining how specific the rubric should be for the end product. The rubric must be detailed enough to provide clear expectations and guidelines but also flexible enough to allow for creativity and individual expression. For instance, while certain elements like vocabulary from the science unit or specific labels might be required, areas such as presentation style or creative aspects can be left open-ended.

Another challenge is when a student or group struggles to decide how to proceed or which tool to use, even after the Inspire phase. In these cases, it's natural for some students to feel indecisive. Teachers can provide more direct guidance or suggest that students revisit their notes from the earlier phases. Alternatively, giving them a sample or idea can offer a starting point without dictating their entire creative process.

Managing and monitoring multiple groups using different digital tools simultaneously can also be tricky. It's helpful to have stations or designated areas for each tool. Assigning roles within groups, such as "project manager," "editor," and "researcher," ensures that each student has a clear responsibility. Regular check-ins, either at set intervals or by moving around the classroom, help monitor progress and provide assistance as needed.

There might be concerns if the final product doesn't meet the expectations or guidelines laid out in the rubric. Providing constructive feedback is essential in these situations. Emphasize what the students did well and where they could improve. If time allows, consider offering an opportunity for revisions. Remember, the goal is not just the end product but also the learning journey they undertake.

Addressing concerns about the quality and accuracy of content in student-created videos can be another hurdle. Ensuring that misconceptions are cleared up during the Expand phase is crucial. Encouraging peer review or group evaluations before the final submission helps maintain accuracy and allows for corrections in case of errors.

Lastly, dealing with students who finish their creations early, or need more time than allocated, can be challenging. For early finishers, provide extension activities or encourage them to help or mentor peers to keep them engaged. If students need more time, consider splitting the activity over multiple sessions or giving them additional time outside regular class hours, if possible.

Create in Action:
Scenario from Ms. Anderson

Ms. Anderson's students spent the next few days working on their storyboards and then bringing their stories to life using the stop-motion app. They created various props and backgrounds using craft supplies.

Ms. Anderson moved around the classroom, observing and offering guidance as needed. "Remember, small movements and steady hands!"

Aiden, now more confident, worked diligently on his animation. "Look, Ms. Anderson! I made the toy jump over a hurdle!"

"That's fantastic, Aiden! You've really improved," Ms. Anderson praised, noting his progress.

Emma and her friend worked on a complex scene involving a toy parade. "This is going to be the best animation ever!" Emma declared, snapping photos carefully.

As Ms. Anderson continued to circulate the room, she noticed that one student, Jake, was struggling with his stop-motion project. His toy character wasn't moving smoothly, and the transitions between scenes felt choppy. Jake looked frustrated, and it was clear he was losing confidence.

Ms. Anderson knelt beside him and watched a few seconds of his animation. "You're doing a great job, Jake. I can see the effort you're putting in. How about we try making the movements just a bit smaller? That way, your animation will look smoother. Let's try it together on the next frame."

With Ms. Anderson's encouragement, Jake adjusted his approach, making more subtle movements between each shot. His animation looked much more fluid as he played back the new frames. Ms. Anderson smiled and said, "See the difference? You're getting the hang of it. Keep going, and remember, patience is key in stop-motion. I'm excited to see how your story turns out!"

Jake nodded with renewed determination, feeling more confident with each frame he captured. The guidance Ms. Anderson provided not only helped Jake improve his project but also reinforced the importance of perseverance and paying attention to detail.

The Create phase is where exploration meets execution. The objective isn't just to produce a product but to let students take charge of their learning, integrate their understanding of the digital tool with the subject matter, and create something unique. It's a celebration of knowledge, creativity, and technological dexterity.

Chapter 11
H for Huddle

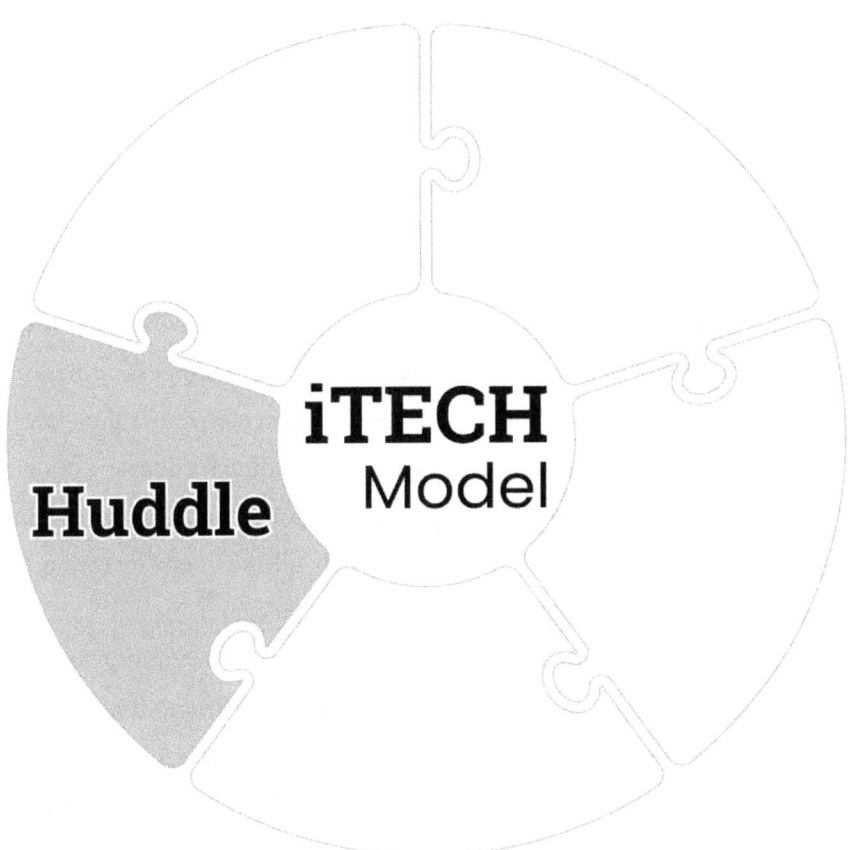

The Huddle phase shifts the focus from individual creation to collective refinement. It promotes the idea that sharing and collaboration are intrinsic to the student's journey. Here, students present their projects, invite constructive feedback, and brainstorm on possible improvements, all while the teacher facilitates and guides this collaborative feedback process.

The objective is to foster an environment where students can share their creations, seek feedback, and collaboratively refine their work for a more polished product, reflecting both individual insights and collective wisdom.

Key Components of the Huddle Phase

The Huddle phase of the iTECH model comprises several key components essential for fostering a supportive and constructive learning environment. Presenting the creation is the first step, where students showcase their work, whether by standing up in class or uploading it to a digital platform. This moment allows students to take pride in their creations and share them with their peers.

Next, receiving and providing feedback is crucial. Peers critically analyze each other's work, highlighting strengths and suggesting areas for improvement. This process not only helps the presenter refine their project but also develops the analytical skills of those providing feedback. Following the feedback, revision comes into play. Students jot down potential enhancements based on the feedback received, which allows them to refine their projects further and learn the value of constructive criticism.

The teacher's role in this phase, while not directly giving feedback, is pivotal in ensuring that the feedback remains constructive and guiding students when they encounter roadblocks. The teacher's oversight helps maintain a positive and productive atmosphere, fostering an environment where students feel safe to express their ideas and grow from the feedback they receive. This combination of presenting, receiving feedback, revising, and teacher guidance makes the Huddle phase a critical component of the iTECH model.

Feedback is a gift. Encourage students to view feedback not as criticism but as a tool for growth. While feedback should be honest, it should also be delivered with kindness and respect.

The teacher can also help the students understand that the first creation is rarely the final product. Iteration based on feedback ensures a more refined outcome. While individual creation is valuable, collective feedback enriches the learning process.

Challenges of the Huddle Phase

Teachers may face several challenges during the Huddle phase of the iTECH model. One common challenge is ensuring students provide constructive feedback without hurting their peers' feelings. To address this issue, it's crucial to set clear guidelines on what constructive feedback looks like. Before the Huddle phase, spend time discussing and role-playing the differences between constructive and destructive criticism. Emphasize the importance of kindness, respect, and focusing on the work rather than the individual. This foundational work can help create a supportive feedback environment.

Another challenge teachers might face is dealing with students who feel overwhelmed with too much feedback. It's natural for some students to feel inundated when multiple peers provide feedback. To help manage this, guide students to prioritize feedback by asking them to categorize suggestions into "must-implement," "consider implementing," and "optional." This approach lets students focus on the most crucial improvements first, making the feedback more manageable and actionable.

Resistance to feedback is another common issue, often stemming from insecurity or fear of judgment. To address this, encourage a classroom culture where mistakes are viewed as learning opportunities. Leading by example can be powerful; share your own work and demonstrate how you receive and integrate feedback. Over time, as students witness the benefits of constructive feedback, their resistance is likely to decrease.

Ensuring every student gets equal attention during the Huddle phase can also be challenging, especially in larger classes. A structured approach can help. Consider breaking students into smaller feedback groups, ensuring each student has a set time to present and receive feedback. For larger projects, using digital platforms like Padlet can allow for asynchronous feedback, ensuring everyone's work is seen and commented on.

Another crucial aspect of the Huddle phase is guiding students to act on the feedback rather than just receiving it. Post-Huddle reflection is key. Ask students to document the feedback they've received and create an action plan. They should note the changes they intend to make based on the feedback, turning feedback into actionable steps rather than just observations.

Finally, teachers may encounter instances where feedback is incorrect or misguided. As a teacher, you're still the facilitator. If you notice feedback that's off the mark, gently correct it. This can be done either in the moment or afterward, depending on the situation. It's also a learning opportunity for the student giving the feedback, helping them refine their critical analysis skills. By addressing these challenges thoughtfully, teachers can make the Huddle phase a productive and enriching part of the iTECH model.

Huddle in Action: Scenario from Ms. Anderson

At the end of the week, Ms. Anderson's students gathered to showcase their completed animations. Ms. Anderson set up a Padlet board where students could upload their videos for everyone to see.

"Who's ready to share their work?" Ms. Anderson asked.

Aiden was the first to volunteer. He played his video on the smartboard, showing his toy's adventure. The class erupted in applause.

"Great job, Aiden!" Ms. Anderson said. "Now, let's give him some feedback. What did you like about his animation?"

"I loved how the toy jumped over the hurdle," said Emma.

"And the camera was really steady," added Lucas.

"Thank you, everyone," Aiden said, beaming with pride.

Each student took their turn presenting, receiving feedback from their peers. Ms. Anderson was amazed at the creativity and effort each student had put into their project.

The Huddle phase underscores the importance of collective insights in refining individual creations. By emphasizing community, feedback, and iterative improvement, this phase teaches students the value of collaboration and receptive communication in any creative journey. It's not just about creating, but refining and redefining, ensuring that their work is a true reflection of their capabilities and the constructive input of their peers.

Section 3

Implementing the iTECH Model

Chapter 12
Implementing the iTECH Model in Various Classroom Settings

The iTECH model is a versatile framework designed to integrate technology into classroom settings to enhance learning across different grade levels, subjects, and student ability levels. By fostering an environment of exploration, creativity, and collaboration, the iTECH model ensures that all students can benefit from digital learning tools tailored to their specific needs. Here, we explore examples of how the iTECH model can be effectively used in diverse educational contexts.

Example 1: Elementary School, First Grade Mathematics

Inspire

Ms. Garcia introduces her first-grade class to a new math app that uses colorful animations to teach basic addition and subtraction. She starts with a short, engaging video of animated characters solving math problems in a magical world, capturing the students' attention and curiosity.

Try

The students are given tablets and five minutes to explore the app on their own. They drag and drop virtual objects to solve simple math equations, discovering how the app works through hands-on experimentation.

Expand

Ms. Garcia brings the class together for a "Tech Talk." She asks the students to share what they discovered about the app. One student mentions a feature where you can get hints if you're stuck, while another talks about how they enjoyed the immediate feedback when they got a problem right. As students shared, Ms. Garcia noticed a recurring misconception: several students believed that the hints provided by the app were the only way to solve difficult problems, leading them to rely too heavily on this feature. They also seemed to think that the immediate feedback only meant they were on the right track rather than an opportunity to deepen their understanding of the problem.

To address these misconceptions, Ms. Garcia explained, "The hints are there to guide you if you're truly stuck, but I encourage you to first try different strategies on your own before turning to the hints. This will help you strengthen your problem-solving skills. Additionally, the immediate feedback isn't just about getting the right answer—it's an opportunity to reflect on why your answer is correct and how you arrived at it. Use it as a moment to understand the problem more deeply."

Ms. Garcia then guided the students through an example problem using the app. She showed them how to approach it without relying on hints and how to use feedback as a tool for deeper learning. By the end of the discussion, students had a clearer understanding of how to use the app more effectively to enhance their learning.

Create

With a clear understanding of the app, the students are now tasked with creating their own simple math problems using the app's tools. They work in pairs to design problems and challenge their classmates to solve them. This activity reinforces their understanding of addition and subtraction while allowing them to use their creativity.

Huddle

The class gathers to showcase their math problems. Each pair presents their challenge, and their classmates attempt to solve it. Feedback is provided, and students note how they could improve their problems for future activities.

Example 2: Middle School, Sixth Grade Science

Inspire

Mr. Thompson's sixth-grade science class is about to start a unit on ecosystems. He begins with a virtual field trip to different biomes using an augmented reality app, showing students various ecosystems around the world and highlighting key features.

Try

Students are given five minutes to explore the app themselves, navigating through different biomes and observing the flora and fauna in each ecosystem. They take notes on interesting features and jot down their questions about the ecosystems.

Expand

The class regroups for a "Tech Talk," where students share their findings. Mr. Thompson notices a few misconceptions. For instance, one student assumes that the lack of trees in the tundra means it is less important than other ecosystems. Another student mistakenly believes all deserts are hot, based on their experience with the app's depiction of the Sahara. Mr.

Thompson uses these misconceptions as teaching moments, explaining that each ecosystem, regardless of its climate or vegetation, plays a crucial role in Earth's biodiversity. He also introduces scientific terms like "biodiversity" and "adaptation" to deepen their understanding.

Create

Students are divided into groups and assigned different ecosystems to research. Using the app and other digital resources, they create multimedia presentations that include images, videos, and interactive elements to explain the characteristics and importance of their assigned ecosystem. The students work collaboratively to create multimedia presentations that include images, videos, and interactive elements to showcase the unique characteristics and significance of their assigned ecosystems. One group, assigned the coral reef ecosystem, creates an interactive timeline of coral bleaching events, while another group, assigned the desert biome, includes a video explaining the role of nocturnal animals in maintaining the ecosystem's balance.

Huddle

Groups present their multimedia projects to the class. Peers provide constructive feedback, highlighting strengths and suggesting improvements. Mr. Thompson facilitates the discussion, ensuring that feedback remains focused on both content and technical skills. He also highlights key learning points, such as the importance of ecosystem conservation, making sure all students grasp the essential concepts before wrapping up the lesson.

Example 3: High School, Tenth Grade History

Inspire

Ms. Lee wants her tenth-grade history students to understand the impact of the Industrial Revolution. She shows them a short documentary clip that overviews the era and its significance.

Try

Students are given access to a historical simulation game that allows them to experience life during the Industrial Revolution. They spend five minutes exploring the game, making choices that affect their virtual characters' lives and industries.

Expand

In the "Tech Talk," students share their experiences from the game. Some discuss the challenges of managing a factory, while others discuss the social changes they observed. Ms. Lee addresses any misconceptions and points out critical historical facts.

Create

Students are asked to write a reflective essay on their experience in the simulation game, comparing it to the actual historical events they have studied. They use digital tools to create timelines and infographics that support their essays.

Huddle

Students share their essays and visual aids with the class. They discuss their insights and receive feedback from peers and Ms. Lee, who helps them refine their arguments and presentations.

Example 4: Mixed Ability Classroom, Third Grade English Language Arts

Inspire

In a third-grade class with diverse learning abilities, Ms. Johnson introduces a digital storytelling app by showing a captivating story created using the app. The story features engaging characters and plot twists, sparking the students' interest.

Try

Students explore the app for five minutes, experimenting with different story elements such as characters, backgrounds, and voice recordings. They begin to understand how to create their own digital stories.

Expand

During the "Tech Talk," students discuss what they found interesting and any difficulties encountered. Ms. Johnson addresses these issues, showing them how to use specific features of the app more effectively.

Create

Each student, according to their ability level, creates a short digital story. Some students work independently, while others collaborate in pairs or small groups. They use the app to write, illustrate, and narrate their stories, focusing on developing their language and storytelling skills.

Huddle

The class gathers to share their digital stories. Each student or group presents their work, and peers provide feedback. Ms. Johnson offers additional insights, praising their creativity and helping them see how they can improve their storytelling techniques.

The versatility of the iTECH model lies in its adaptability. Whether you're teaching kindergarten math or fifth-grade literature, the model can be tailored to offer engaging, tech-integrated learning experiences to all students.

By adapting the iTECH model to different grade levels, subjects, and student ability levels, educators can create engaging, effective learning experiences. These lessons will harness the power of technology to foster creativity, critical thinking, and collaboration.

Chapter 13
Adapting the iTECH Model for Different Subject Areas

In today's schools, it's paramount for educators to be at the forefront of integrating technology into teaching and learning. The iTECH model offers a structured pathway to achieve this goal. However, introducing technology in an isolated lesson or subject isn't sufficient to prepare students for a world that's deeply interwoven with technology. There's immense value in consistent technology integration across all subjects. When technology becomes an integral part of the curriculum, it does more than just enhance the subject at hand; it fosters essential life skills. Understanding digital literacy, online collaboration, and adaptive problem-solving become second nature to students.

Integrating technology uniformly ensures that students see and understand its ubiquitous nature, reinforcing the idea that the digital tools they use aren't just confined to a particular subject but are versatile instruments capable of enhancing their overall learning experience. This consistent approach also ensures that all students, irrespective of their preferred subjects, get equal exposure to technology, equipping them with vital skills for the future.

While the iTECH model offers a universally applicable framework for integrating technology into teaching, it's essential to tailor its implementation to meet the needs of different subject areas, grade levels, and learning needs. Here's how you can use the iTECH model in various subjects:

Mathematics

The iTECH model can be specifically tailored for mathematics education by leveraging a variety of digital tools that enhance students' understanding and engagement with mathematical concepts.

Inspire

Begin by demonstrating real-world applications of math using digital tools. For example, you could show how architects use geometry in designing buildings with GeoGebra or how data analysts use graphs to make decisions using Desmos.

Try

Allow students to experiment with math apps like Photomath or Mathway to input complex equations and visualize solutions. Let them use Desmos to plot functions or GeoGebra to create geometric shapes and explore their properties. Encourage them to use AR and VR tools to make abstract concepts tangible, such as visualizing three-dimensional shapes or understanding calculus concepts through interactive simulations.

Expand

Facilitate group discussions where students share their experiences with these tools. They can discuss how Photomath helped them understand a difficult equation or how they used GeoGebra to discover the properties of a geometric shape. Highlight the mathematical principles behind these tools and their applications.

Create

Encourage students to create their own math models or graphs using Desmos or GeoGebra. They can design a project that requires them to apply their mathematical knowledge. For example, they can create a digital representation of a real-world problem or animating a mathematical concept using these platforms.

Huddle

In a collaborative setting, have students present their creations and discuss the challenges they faced and the solutions they found. Peer feedback can help refine their understanding and approach. Use platforms like Padlet or Google Classroom to share their work and gather feedback from a wider audience.

By adapting the iTECH model for mathematics, educators can make abstract concepts more tangible and encourage problem-solving and critical thinking. They can also provide students with tools that make learning math an engaging and interactive experience.

The Geometry of Architecture

Inspire

Mrs. Reynolds kicks off the lesson with a short video showcasing the world's most innovative buildings, which emphasizes their unique geometric designs.

Try

Students are then introduced to an app that lets them design basic architectural sketches. They're allowed a few minutes to explore and draw random structures, familiarizing themselves with the tools.

Expand

After the exploration, students discuss their findings. Mrs. Reynolds highlights essential tools on the app and introduces the challenge: designing a sustainable house using specific geometric shapes.

Create

Students, working in teams, develop their architectural designs, keeping geometric constraints in mind.

Huddle

Designs are shared on a digital platform where peers can comment. Feedback revolves around the integration of geometry in the designs and the aesthetics of the structure.

Language Arts

Websites like Storybird or tools like Adobe Express can be employed as digital storytelling tools. After familiarizing themselves during the Try phase, students can create their own digital stories or poems. Platforms like Epic! or Audible can be used for listening to or reading stories, followed by discussions or creative assignments. Tools like Grammarly or games like 'Grammar Gorillas' help students enhance their grammar in a playful manner.

In the Expand phase, discuss language structures or literary techniques highlighted by the tech tool.

The World of Digital Storytelling

Inspire

Mr. Thompson starts by reading a gripping excerpt from a mystery novel. He then showcases a digital story created by students in another class.

Try

Students get a hands-on introduction to a digital storytelling platform where they explore various features, from character design to dialogue boxes.

Expand

They share unique features they discovered. Mr. Thompson then provides a structure for their story, introduces plot elements, and shares a rubric for the assignment.

Create

Students craft their short digital mystery stories, ensuring they hit all the elements of the plot.

Huddle

Stories are shared, and peers provide feedback, focusing on plot development and creativity.

Science

Websites like the PhET Interactive Simulations allow students to conduct experiments in a digital space. This eliminates physical constraints and hazards. During the Create phase, using a digital lab, students could use a digital microscope app to examine and document various specimens.

Platforms such as Starry Night Education can be used to explore astronomical phenomena or simulate space missions. Apps like Arduino Science Journal can turn a device into a pocket laboratory, measuring light, sound, and more.

Virtual Journey to the Stars

Inspire

Mrs. Anderson starts with breathtaking images of constellations and planets. She asks, "How might we travel through space without leaving our classroom?"

Try

Students are introduced to a virtual reality space exploration app. They spend time navigating through stars, planets, and galaxies.

Expand

Post-exploration, students share unique celestial objects they encountered. Mrs. Anderson highlights critical regions of our solar system and beyond.

Create

Students are tasked with mapping a journey through space, as well as highlighting and researching at least five celestial objects.

Huddle

Virtual space journeys are shared, and students provide feedback on the chosen path and information accuracy.

Social Studies

Google Earth or Arts & Culture can transport students to historical sites or geographic landmarks, allowing in-depth exploration without leaving the classroom. Tools like Time.Graphics enable students to create and explore detailed timelines and visualize historical events in context. Platforms like iCivics offer games and lessons to immerse students in civic topics, enhancing their understanding of political processes. Incorporate virtual field trips or historical simulation games. In the Create phase, students could virtually rebuild historical landmarks using design software.

Ancient Civilizations Come to Life

Inspire

Mr. Khan showcases artifacts from the ancient Indus Valley civilization and plays an AR-enhanced video that brings the civilization to life.

Try

Students get access to an augmented reality (AR) app that overlays historical data onto real-world objects. They spend time exploring various civilizations.

Expand

They share their unique discoveries. Mr. Khan provides context, explaining the significance of different ancient civilizations.

Create

Students pick a civilization and create an AR-based presentation that would educate someone unfamiliar with that era.

Huddle

AR presentations are showcased, with feedback centered on historical accuracy and AR integration.

Physical Education and Arts

Applications like GarageBand for music or Dance Reality for dance help students create and understand compositions, rhythm, and choreography. Tools like Procreate or Adobe Fresco provide students with a canvas to explore digital art techniques and styles. Explore digital painting tools or music composition apps. The Huddle phase might involve students critiquing each other's digital artworks. Leveraging apps like MyFitnessPal or Fitbit in PE classes can teach students about health metrics and promote physical activity.

Dance Meets Technology

Inspire

Coach Williams displays a digital dance choreographed by professionals using motion-capture technology.

Try

Students are given motion-sensing bands and access to dance

composition software. They move and see their motions translated into digital dance moves.

Expand

The discussion revolves around different dance moves they could create. Coach Williams then introduces a dance challenge.

Create

In groups, students choreograph a short digital dance sequence integrating at least ten different moves.

Huddle

Dance sequences are showcased. Feedback centers on creativity and the fluency of the moves.

While the iTECH model promotes universal skills, its adaptability allows it to be embedded seamlessly into different subjects. By combining the structure of the iTECH model with discipline-specific tools and platforms, educators can create enriched learning experiences.

By aligning the iTECH model with subject-specific tools, educators can create a cohesive learning environment where technology amplifies the subject matter, making lessons more interactive, engaging, and effective.

Chapter 14
Grade-Level Adaptations

The iTECH model, which focuses on student exploration and technological integration, is inherently adaptable. However, the way it's executed needs to align with the cognitive and developmental stages of different age groups. Here's a breakdown of how to adapt the iTECH Model for primary, intermediate, middle, and high school students:

Primary Level (K-2)

At this early stage, simplicity and engagement are key. Young students need clear, basic instructions and vibrant, interactive elements to capture their attention and foster learning.

Inspire

Start with bright visuals and storytelling. Use animated videos or colorful presentations that relate to the technology tool or topic—for example, showing a short, engaging cartoon that introduces the concept of coding through a story about a character navigating a digital world.

Try

Ensure that the digital tools are age-appropriate with intuitive, user-friendly interfaces. Apps with drag-and-drop features, vibrant visuals, and gamified elements are ideal. For instance, use a basic drawing app where students can create pictures by dragging and dropping shapes.

Expand

Create a fun and relaxed sharing environment. Consider 'show and tell' sessions where students demonstrate what they learned. Use props and physical aids to highlight new words or technical terms, such as colorful flashcards with images.

Create

Keep projects short and visually stimulating. Activities could include creating a simple digital poster, a brief animation, or recording a short audio clip. Encourage creativity without overwhelming them with lengthy assignments.

Huddle

Use playful peer review methods. Turn feedback sessions into games where students highlight one thing they liked and one suggestion for improvement in their peer's project. This will make the process engaging and less intimidating.

Intermediate Level (3-5)

At this stage, students can handle slightly more complex tasks and are capable of deeper understanding and longer attention spans.

Inspire

Utilize more detailed visuals and interactive storytelling. Present animated videos or interactive stories that introduce the technology tool or concept in an engaging way, like a short documentary about how robots are used in everyday life.

Try

Introduce slightly more sophisticated tools that still maintain a user-friendly interface. Use educational games or apps that challenge their problem-solving skills, such as a simple coding platform where they can program a character to complete tasks.

Expand

Foster a dynamic sharing environment. Use digital platforms where students can upload and present their findings. Introduce technical terms with visual aids and encourage students to explain them in their own words during the "Tech Talk."

Create

Projects can be more detailed, such as creating a digital storybook, a short video, or a simple slideshow presentation. Encourage students to incorporate multimedia elements like images, sound, and text to make their projects more engaging.

Huddle

Implement structured peer review sessions. Have students work in pairs or small groups to provide constructive feedback. Teach them how to give and receive feedback positively and use it to make improvements to their projects.

By tailoring the iTECH model to suit the cognitive and developmental capacities of students at various grade levels, educators can ensure that technological integration is both effective and age appropriate. This care provides students with a continuous learning trajectory, building on their technological fluency as they progress through their schooling.

Middle School (6-8)

Middle school students can engage with more complex tools and concepts, and they benefit from collaborative and critical thinking activities.

Inspire

Use sophisticated multimedia presentations or video clips. Start discussions with open-ended questions to pique curiosity and stimulate critical thinking, such as a video on the impact of technology on society followed by a discussion on its pros and cons.

Try

Introduce tools with a learning curve that allows for deeper exploration. Platforms for basic coding, digital design, or simulation games are ideal. For instance, use a simple website builder or a coding app where students can create their own games.

Expand

Encourage group discussions and brainstorming sessions. Integrate more technical language, ensuring that new terms are clearly explained with examples. Use collaborative platforms where students can share ideas and work on projects together in real time.

Create

Projects can be more comprehensive, such as creating a digital story, building a basic website, or developing a mini game. Encourage students to plan their projects before execution, teaching them the importance of organization and forethought in digital creation.

Huddle

Emphasize constructive criticism and self-evaluation. Teach students to document feedback and use it for future reference. Create opportunities for students to reflect on their learning process and the challenges they faced, helping them to grow from the experience.

By tailoring the iTECH model to different grade levels, educators can effectively engage students in meaningful, technology-enhanced learning experiences that promote creativity, critical thinking, and collaboration.

High School (9-12)

Leverage advanced software, from graphic design to coding platforms. The Expand phase can delve deeper into tech functions, while the Create phase can involve complex, multi-stage projects.

Inspire
Begin with real-world examples. Discuss the relevance of the technology or topic in current events or in potential future careers.

Try
Tools can be professional-grade or industry-standard, like advanced coding platforms, digital design software, or data analysis tools.

Expand
Facilitate in-depth discussions. Encourage students to research independently and share findings. Technical terminology should be fully integrated.

Create
Projects should be multi-faceted and could span multiple days or weeks. This could be creating a mobile app, a digital campaign, or an in-depth research project using data analysis tools.

Huddle
Feedback becomes more formalized. Peer reviews, self-assessments,

and even external feedback (from industry professionals or online communities) can be incorporated.

By tailoring the iTECH Model to suit the cognitive and developmental capacities of students at various grade levels, educators can ensure that technological integration is both effective and age appropriate. This care provides students with a continuous learning trajectory, building on their technological fluency as they progress through their schooling.

Sample Project for 1st Grade: Digital Storybook

Objective: Introduce young students to digital creation tools by creating a simple digital storybook.

Project Title: My First Digital Storybook

Phases

Inspire

Show students an animated storybook created using a digital tool like Book Creator. For example, a short story about a day in the life of a character they know, like a friendly dog or a magical fairy. Discuss the story and ask students what they liked about it.

Try

Allow students to explore the Book Creator app on tablets. Provide them with a basic tutorial on how to add pictures, draw, and type text. Let them spend a few minutes trying out these features independently.

Expand

Facilitate a class discussion where students share what they discovered during their exploration. Highlight important features such as how to change the background, add drawings, or record their voice.

Create

Students create their own simple storybook. They can draw pictures and write a sentence on each page about their favorite animal or a memorable day. Assist them as needed but encourage them to try things on their own.

Huddle

Have a "story time" where students present their digital storybook to the class. Peers provide positive feedback, saying one thing they liked about the story. Encourage students to be supportive and celebrate each other's work.

Expected Outcome: A short digital storybook with drawings and simple sentences that each student created themselves.

Sample Project for 4th Grade: Digital Poster on Endangered Animals

Objective: Develop research and presentation skills using digital tools to create an informative and visually engaging poster.

Project Title: Save the Endangered Animals

Phases

Inspire

Show students a compelling digital poster about endangered animals created using Canva. Discuss the importance of protecting endangered species and what makes a good informative poster.

Try

Let students explore Canva on their computers. Provide them with a brief tutorial on how to use the templates, add text and images, and change colors. Allow them a few minutes to experiment with these features.

Expand

Conduct a "Tech Talk" where students share what they learned about using Canva. Discuss key features they discovered and clarify any misconceptions. Introduce them to additional features like adding infographics or using the search function to find images.

Create

Students choose an endangered animal to research and create a digital poster. They should include facts about the animal, reasons for its endangered status, and ways people can help protect it. Encourage creativity in the design, but ensure they include all necessary information.

Huddle

Organize a gallery walk where students display their posters on the classroom walls or on a shared digital platform like Padlet. Students leave comments or sticky notes with positive feedback and suggestions for improvement. Provide an opportunity for revisions based on feedback received.

Expected Outcome: A detailed and visually appealing digital poster about an endangered animal, demonstrating students' research and design skills.

These sample projects illustrate how the iTECH model can be adapted to suit different grade levels, subjects, and student abilities, fostering creativity, critical thinking, and collaboration in the digital classroom.

Sample Project for 7th Grade: Stop-Motion Animation on Historical Events

Objective: Enhance understanding of historical events and develop technical skills through creating a stop-motion animation.

Project Title: Bringing History to Life with Stop-Motion Animation

Phases

Inspire

Show students a short stop-motion animation depicting a significant historical event created using a digital storytelling tool like Stop Motion Studio. Discuss the event and the techniques used in the animation.

Try

Allow students to explore the Stop Motion Studio app on tablets or computers. Provide a brief tutorial on how to take photos, adjust frame rates, and add audio. Let them experiment by creating a simple animation, like making a character move across the screen.

Expand

Facilitate a "Tech Talk" where students share their experiences with the app. Highlight effective techniques and address common challenges. Introduce additional features like adding sound effects or adjusting animation speed.

Create

Students work in groups to choose a historical event they have studied and create a stop-motion animation depicting the event. They should write a storyboard, create props or use digital images, and record narration or dialogue. Encourage them to focus on key moments of the event to create a coherent and engaging animation.

Huddle

Host a screening session where each group presents their animation to the class. Students provide constructive feedback on each other's work, focusing on both the content and technical aspects of the animation. Encourage groups to revise and improve their animations based on the feedback received.

Expected Outcome

A short stop-motion animation that accurately and creatively represents a historical event, demonstrating students' understanding and technical skills.

These sample projects illustrate how the iTECH model can be adapted to suit different grade levels, subjects, and student abilities, fostering creativity, critical thinking, and collaboration in the digital classroom.

Chapter 15
Diverse Learning Needs

Every classroom is a tapestry of diverse learners, each with unique strengths, challenges, and backgrounds. The iTECH model, being student-centered, offers a robust framework that can be modified to serve all students, ensuring that technology is used as a bridge, not a barrier.

Ms. Anderson and Digital Stop Motion

Ms. Anderson's approach to the iTECH model for creating digital stop-motion animations demonstrated her adeptness in differentiating instruction to meet her students' varying needs. She adapted each phase of the model so all her students could be successful.

Inspire

Ms. Anderson used a visually stimulating and narrative-driven animated video to spark curiosity and interest. For students who are visual learners or those who need more engagement to capture their attention, this method was particularly effective. She was aware that not all students respond to text-heavy introductions, so the video provided an accessible entry point for everyone.

Try

Recognizing that her students had different levels of familiarity with technology, Ms. Anderson allowed them to explore the stop-motion tool independently. For students who might feel overwhelmed, she ensured the tool was simple and intuitive. She circulated the room to offer support to those who struggled, providing additional hints and encouragement. Meanwhile, she allowed advanced students to dive deeper into the tool's features, encouraging them to experiment with more complex functionalities.

Expand

During the Tech Talk, Ms. Anderson ensured every student had the opportunity to share their discoveries. She used a structured approach to manage this, such as having students first share in pairs before discussing as a whole class. This method catered to students who might be shy or reluctant to speak in front of the entire group. For students who needed more time to process their thoughts, the smaller group discussions provided a less intimidating platform to voice their ideas.

Create

In the Create phase, Ms. Anderson set clear but flexible expectations. She provided a rubric that outlined essential elements, like including key vocabulary and ensuring narrative coherence, but allowed students the freedom to express their creativity. For students who needed more guidance, Ms. Anderson offered one-on-one support and additional resources like storyboard templates. For those who were more independent, she encouraged them to push boundaries by incorporating advanced techniques like sound effects or intricate scene transitions.

Huddle

Ms. Anderson facilitated a supportive and constructive feedback session. She emphasized positive reinforcement and specific, actionable feedback, teaching students how to provide and receive constructive criticism. Ms.

Anderson also used a mixture of verbal feedback and written notes to cater to different learning preferences. For students who were more sensitive to critique, she ensured the feedback was framed positively and constructively. Her strategy helped them see it as a tool for growth rather than criticism.

Overall, Ms. Anderson's differentiation within the iTECH model ensured that each student could engage with the material at their level of ability and comfort, fostering an inclusive and supportive learning environment. This thoughtful adaptation not only addressed diverse learning needs but also encouraged all students to develop their technical and creative skills at their own pace.

The adaptability of the iTECH model means it can work for all students: those with disabilities, English language learners, and gifted students.

Students with Disabilities

For students with physical disabilities, opt for assistive tech tools that cater to their specific needs. For instance, during the Try phase, use voice-to-text software for students with motor difficulties.

For students with learning differences, such as ADHD or dyslexia, choose adaptive tech platforms with text customization or built-in focus aids. The Expand phase can involve strategies tailored for attention retention. Let's explore how each phase can be tailored for students with disabilities.

Inspire

Use multimedia resources with subtitles, audio descriptions, or tactile feedback. Ensure all videos are captioned and that content is available in alternative formats like Braille or large print.

Try

Introduce assistive technologies like screen readers, voice-to-text software, or adaptive keyboards/mice. Apps with customizable User Interfaces (UIs) or those that adhere to universal design principles can be beneficial.

Expand

Allow students to communicate their discoveries in various ways such as through speech, sign language, or Augmentative and Alternative Communication (AAC) devices.

Create

Ensure digital tools offer various ways to showcase understanding. For instance, a student might use an app to create a digital storyboard rather than typing a report.

Huddle

Create a feedback environment that values different perspectives. Employ peer buddies or mentors for supportive feedback.

English Language Learners (ELL)

Use translation tools or platforms that offer multi-language support. The Huddle phase can include peer support, where bilingual students help ELLs understand and refine their creations. Here's how to adapt each phase.

Inspire

Use visuals extensively. Videos or presentations can be paired with bilingual subtitles. Incorporate culturally diverse content to make connections.

Try

Tools that offer language support or translation features can be beneficial. Visual-heavy or intuitive UIs can reduce language barriers.

Expand

Encourage sharing in both their native language and English. Use tech to instantly translate and share findings with the class.

Create

Allow projects that incorporate bilingual elements. A digital story could be bilingual, fostering both language appreciation and learning.

Huddle

Feedback can be multi-lingual. Encourage peers to use visual or symbolic feedback methods, reducing language barriers.

Gifted Students

Provide extensions for the tools or have the students use more advanced ones. During the Create phase, set more intricate challenges, or ask them to combine multiple tools. Let's look at how to adapt the iTECH model for gifted students at each phase.

Inspire

Introduce advanced real-world scenarios or challenge them with complex questions to pique their interest.

Try

Offer them advanced tools or platforms that cater to their accelerated learning pace, allowing deeper exploration or multi-layered challenges.

Expand

Encourage them to delve deeper into technical details or to explore ancillary topics related to the main tool or subject. They could act as 'tech mentors' during this phase.

Create

Propose advanced projects or allow them to integrate multiple tools or platforms for a comprehensive solution.

Huddle

Encourage them to provide in-depth feedback, not just on the content but also on the technology used. They could be peer coaches, offering advanced tips.

By embracing the iTECH model's flexibility and merging it with a plethora of available digital tools and platforms, educators can create an inclusive, dynamic, and effective learning environment. Each student, regardless of their unique learning needs, can then harness the power of technology to elevate their learning journey.

Section 4
Evaluating the iTECH Model

Chapter 16
Tools for Assessing the Impact of Technology on Student Learning

Within the context of integrating technology into the learning process, assessment is a crucial component that helps educators gauge student understanding and mastery of skills. Assessments are not one-size-fits-all; they vary in purpose, timing, and format. To better appreciate how we can effectively evaluate students' growth in creativity, critical thinking, and problem-solving, it's essential to understand two primary assessment types: formative and summative.

Formative assessments are akin to checkpoints or pit-stops in a student's learning journey. They are ongoing evaluations that take place during the learning process that offer both the teacher and student immediate feedback. Their primary purpose isn't to grade students but to diagnose where they are and guide instruction accordingly. By giving a real-time pulse check on student understanding, formative assessments allow educators to adjust their teaching strategies, address misconceptions, and offer targeted support.

Summative assessments come at the end of a learning period or unit and provide a culminating measure of a student's understanding or skill proficiency. Think of them as the "final show" where students demonstrate their accumulated knowledge and competencies. These evaluations are typically used for grading purposes, capturing a student's performance at a particular point in time.

While both assessments serve distinct roles, they share a collective goal: ensuring students are equipped with the necessary skills and knowledge, especially in our increasingly digital age. As we delve deeper into strategies tailored for our tech-integrated classrooms, remember that both formative and summative assessments offer valuable insights, as they guide us to create enriching, effective learning experiences for our students.

We're not just assessing the regurgitation of facts or rote memorization. Instead, we aim to measure more abstract yet fundamental skills: creativity, critical thinking, and problem-solving, especially within digital contexts. Each of these competencies are multidimensional and play a vital role in preparing students for a rapidly evolving, interconnected world. Let's delve deeper into the objectives behind assessing each of these skills:

Creativity in a Digital Context: Creativity isn't merely about artistic talents. Within a digital context, creativity refers to the ability of students to generate, explore, and express original ideas using digital tools, fostering innovation and uniqueness. Our goal is to assess how students harness digital platforms to craft distinctive outputs, whether they're designing multimedia projects, developing digital stories, or curating unique content. By assessing creativity, we aim to understand a student's capacity to think divergently, connect disparate ideas, and bring to life imaginative solutions using technology.

Critical Thinking: Critical thinking in the digital realm means the ability to analyze, evaluate, and synthesize information from diverse digital sources. It also means discerning the credibility, relevance, and value of digital content. The focus here is on gauging students' capacities to dissect digital information, question its authenticity, draw meaningful inferences, and make informed decisions based on their digital research. Assessing critical thinking helps educators understand a student's readiness to face the vast, often overwhelming, world of online information with discernment and intelligence.

Problem-Solving Within Digital Environments: Problem-solving refers to a student's aptitude to identify challenges, especially those that emerge in digital tasks or projects, and devise effective solutions. This skill involves both analytical abilities and practical application. We aim to evaluate how students navigate challenges in technology use, software intricacies, and even digital group dynamics. Can they troubleshoot a tech glitch? Can they find alternative ways to achieve a digital task when faced with obstacles? By assessing this skill, we grasp a student's resilience, adaptability, and innovative approach when confronted with digital dilemmas.

Establishing clear objectives for what we're measuring is foundational. These guideposts ensure our assessment strategies are aligned with our educational goals which allows us to truly comprehend our students' readiness and adaptability in an ever-evolving digital world.

Digital Tools for Formative Assessment

Incorporating technology into the classroom has undoubtedly transformed the educational landscape, offering a multitude of avenues for assessing student learning. When it comes to formative assessment – that continuous, in-the-moment check on student understanding – a range of digital tools provides educators with immediate feedback, fostering adaptability in teaching methods and tailoring lessons to individual student needs. Let's explore some of these powerful tools:

1. Quizzes & Polls

- **Platform Features:** The age of paper quizzes has evolved into a dynamic, interactive, and often game-like experience. Platforms like Kahoot allow teachers to create lively quiz competitions, making learning and assessment a fun process. Quizlet offers engaging study sets and games, while Google Forms provides a customizable platform to create quizzes and instantly gather student responses.

- **Benefits:** These tools not only gauge student comprehension in real time but also offer instant feedback to students, enhancing their grasp of concepts. Teachers can quickly identify gaps in understanding, making timely instructional adjustments.

2. Interactive Platforms

- **Platform Features:** Interactivity is at the core of student engagement. Tools like Padlet provide a digital canvas for students to post thoughts, questions, or multimedia, serving as an evolving bulletin board of ideas.

- **Benefits:** Such platforms capture the dynamism of student thought, allowing teachers to see patterns, spark discussions, and encourage collaborative learning. It shifts assessment from passive reception to active participation.

3. Digital Journals/Blogs

- **Platform Features:** The reflective nature of journaling finds a new dimension in the digital world. Seesaw is a student-driven platform where youngsters can create a portfolio of their work, including videos, photos, and documents, chronicling their learning journey. For older students, Edublogs offers the opportunity to hone writing skills, develop a digital voice, and engage in thoughtful reflection through blogging.

- **Benefits:** Digital journals and blogs not only serve as a repository of student work but also as a window into their evolving thought processes, self-assessments, and personal growth. These platforms foster a deeper metacognitive understanding, allowing educators to understand student perspectives, challenges, and achievements over time.

Ms. Anderson's approach to assessing her students throughout the digital stop-motion animation project was comprehensive and integrated both formative and summative assessments using various digital tools. Here's how she did her formative assessments:

1. Initial Exploration with Digital Tools

- **Tool Used:** Google Forms
- **Method:** After the Inspire phase, Ms. Anderson asked students to complete a short Google Forms survey to gauge their initial understanding and excitement about the project. The form included questions like, "What did you find most interesting about the animation you saw?" and "What do you think you need to learn to create your own animation?"
- **Purpose:** This helped Ms. Anderson understand students' baseline knowledge and identify any misconceptions or areas that needed further clarification.

2. During the Try Phase

- **Tool Used:** Padlet
- **Method:** As students experimented with the digital storytelling tool, they posted their discoveries and questions on a shared Padlet board. This allowed Ms. Anderson to monitor their progress and see common challenges or successes.
- **Purpose:** The real-time feedback from Padlet enabled Ms. Anderson

to provide timely assistance and adjust her instructions to better meet students' needs.

3. Interactive Feedback Sessions

- **Tool Used:** Flip (This platform no longer exists. However, some platforms with similar features include Padlet or using Vimeo to record videos and then post to Waklet.)

- **Method:** Throughout the project, students recorded short video reflections on Flip, discussing what they had learned and any difficulties encountered. Peers could view and respond to these reflections, fostering a collaborative learning environment.

- **Purpose:** This ongoing reflection helped students internalize their learning. It also provided Ms. Anderson with insights into their thought processes and problem-solving strategies.

Leveraging these digital tools for formative assessment ensures that both educators and students are in sync, enhancing the teaching-learning process. They provide immediate insights, making education more responsive, personalized, and engaging.

Digital Tools for Summative Assessment

In our modern, technologically advanced classrooms, summative assessments – those conclusive evaluations that sum up a student's understanding at the end of an instructional unit – have also evolved. They're no longer just about paper-pencil tests. Now, we have the advantage of a myriad of digital tools that not only assess the endpoint but also capture the breadth and depth of a student's journey. Here's how these tools are enhancing summative assessment:

1. Digital Portfolios

- **Platform Features:** A digital portfolio is like a personal academic museum, showcasing the growth, accomplishments, and talents of students. Platforms such as Portfoliobox allow students to exhibit a rich tapestry of their work, including essays, art, and digital projects. Google Sites provides an intuitive way for students to build a comprehensive website, compiling their academic achievements and reflections in one place.

- **Benefits:** Digital portfolios offer a holistic view of a student's skills and knowledge. They highlight not just the final product but also the thought process, revisions, and iterations behind it. For educators, it provides a comprehensive assessment tool that goes beyond mere grades, capturing growth over time.

2. Multimedia Presentations

- **Platform Features:** The days of bland, textual slides are long gone. Today's students have the advantage of dynamic tools like PowerPoint, with its advanced design and animation features. Prezi offers a non-linear, visually engaging presentation format, and Canva is perfect for infographics and visually rich slides.

- **Benefits:** Using these tools for summative assessment allows students to demonstrate their grasp of content in innovative and personal ways. It tests their ability to synthesize, design, and communicate. For educators, it's a chance to see the depth of understanding and the creativity of expression.

3. Simulations & Virtual Labs

- **Platform Features:** Theoretical knowledge gets a real-world context with simulations and virtual labs. Students can apply their learning in controlled, virtual environments, experimenting, making mistakes, and learning from them.

- **Benefits:** These digital platforms are game-changers for assessing problem-solving skills. Students can be presented with real-time challenges or scenarios that test their application of concepts. For educators, it provides insights into students' analytical thinking, decision-making processes, and hands-on application of knowledge.

Here are Ms. Anderson's summative assessments:

1. Final Project Submission

- **Tool Used:** Google Classroom
- **Method:** Students submitted their completed stop-motion animations through Google Classroom. The submission included the final video, a written reflection on their creative process, and a peer review form.
- **Purpose:** Google Classroom streamlined the collection of student work and allowed for easy distribution of feedback.

2. Digital Rubric for Evaluation

- **Tool Used:** Rubric Maker integrated with Google Classroom
- **Method:** Ms. Anderson created a detailed rubric using Rubric Maker, which she shared with students at the beginning of the project. The rubric assessed various aspects such as creativity, technical skills, adherence to the storyline, and the use of digital tools.
- **Purpose:** The rubric provided clear expectations and a consistent framework for evaluating each student's work.

3. Peer Review and Feedback:

- **Tool Used:** Padlet and Google Docs

- **Method:** Students posted their animations on a Padlet board, where peers could leave comments and constructive feedback. Additionally, they used Google Docs to fill out peer review forms, highlighting strengths and suggesting improvements.

- **Purpose:** This peer review process encouraged critical thinking and allowed students to engage in constructive dialogue about each other's work.

Incorporating these digital tools for summative assessment not only provides a richer, more nuanced understanding of students' capabilities but also ensures that assessments are more engaging, interactive, and reflective of real-world contexts.

Combining Digital Assessment Tools:

- **Integrated Reflection:** Ms. Anderson used a combination of Google Forms, Flip, and Google Docs to gather student reflections at different stages of the project. This technology provided a comprehensive view of their learning journey.

- **Real-time Feedback and Monitoring:** Using Padlet and Google Classroom allowed for continuous monitoring and feedback, ensuring that students stayed on track and received the support they needed.

- **Consistent Evaluation:** The detailed rubric created with Rubric Maker ensured all students were evaluated consistently, and Google Classroom facilitated the efficient distribution of feedback.

Through these digital assessment tools, Ms. Anderson was able to provide ongoing, formative feedback while also assessing her students' final products. This ensured a holistic approach to their learning and development.

Feedback Mechanisms

1. **Collaborative Document Editing:** Platforms like Google Docs or Microsoft Word Online enable teachers to leave real-time comments on student work. This feature facilitates a continuous feedback loop, allowing students to make adjustments as they work.

2. **Digital Peer Review:** Tools such as Peergrade allow students to provide feedback on each other's assignments. Peer assessments can offer diverse perspectives and reinforce learning.

3. **Screen Recording Feedback:** Instead of written comments, teachers can use tools like Loom or Screencastify to record their feedback while reviewing a student's digital project. This method can be more personal and in-depth.

4. **Self-Assessment Tools:** Encourage students to reflect on their work using digital self-assessment tools. Digital forms or surveys can prompt students to think about what they learned, the challenges they faced, and areas for improvement.

5. **Digital Badges and Micro-Credentials:** Platforms like Canvas Badges or Credly can be used to award digital badges to students, acknowledging their achievements and competencies in specific areas.

Assessment and feedback in a technology-rich environment move beyond traditional paper-and-pencil tests. The digital age provides a plethora of tools to make the evaluation process more interactive, immediate, and insightful. When effectively integrated into the iTECH model, these tools not only assess knowledge but also skills like collaboration, critical thinking, and technological proficiency. The key is to choose the tools that best align with the learning objectives and the nature of the digital task while ensuring that feedback remains constructive and encourages growth.

For students, the iTECH model doesn't just mean learning how to use a tool or software; it's about gaining the skills and mindset to navigate the digital frontier with confidence. The long-term benefits are profound. With consistent application of the model, students are poised to transition from passive consumers to active creators. They are equipped not just with technological proficiency but also with the critical thinking, creativity, and collaboration skills that are paramount in almost every future career and personal endeavor.

Chapter 17
Measuring Student Learning

Setting the stage for any assessment or evaluation involves a clear-eyed look at what we aim to achieve. By establishing lucid objectives and benchmarks, we can systematically track our progress, make informed decisions, and ensure that our efforts align with our broader educational goals. This foundational step is particularly crucial when integrating innovations like the iTECH model and other educational technologies into the classroom.

Objectives serve as our compass, pointing us in the direction we intend to go. Without them, we risk venturing off course or losing sight of our purpose. When we talk about integrating a model like iTECH or leveraging new educational technology tools, the objectives illuminate the purpose behind our choices. Are we looking to foster better student collaboration, enhance their critical thinking abilities, or make learning experiences more engaging and tailored to individual needs? By articulating these goals, we ensure that every step taken aligns with our overarching mission.

To define clear objectives, begin with broad educational goals. Perhaps you want to enhance student engagement, improve academic performance, or cultivate 21st-century skills. From these broad strokes, distill specific, measurable objectives. For instance, an objective might be to increase student participation in group projects by 20% or to enhance students' abilities to critically evaluate digital sources.

While objectives outline what we hope to achieve, benchmarks provide specific checkpoints or standards against which we can measure our progress. They transform our objectives from abstract concepts into concrete, measurable targets. For the iTECH model, benchmarks might include specific proficiency levels on tech tools, desired scores on digital literacy assessments, or certain engagement metrics on digital platforms.

It's essential to understand that our objectives for integrating the iTECH model and educational technology will evolve. As the digital landscape shifts and our educational environment changes, our goals too will need periodic reassessment and adjustment. By establishing a routine of revisiting and refining our objectives and benchmarks, we ensure that our educational strategies remain relevant, effective, and aligned with our students' changing needs.

Clear objectives and benchmarks are not mere formalities but the bedrock upon which successful integration of the iTECH model and educational technology stands. By grounding our efforts in well-defined goals and measurable standards, we set the stage for meaningful progress, informed decision-making, and impactful educational outcomes.

Quantitative Metrics

When measuring the success of the iTECH model and the impact of innovative educational technology, numbers speak volumes. Quantitative metrics offer a tangible way to gauge the outcomes of our initiatives, providing clear, data-driven insights into what's working and where adjustments might be needed. These hard numbers, while not the whole story, play an indispensable role in painting a holistic picture of our efforts' impact.

1. **Student Performance:** The ultimate objective of any educational model or tool is to enhance student learning. One of the most direct ways to gauge this is by monitoring shifts in student performance by

using the following:

- **Test Scores:** By comparing test scores before and after implementing the iTECH model or a particular ed-tech tool, educators can identify if there's been a tangible boost in understanding and knowledge retention.

- **Assignment Grades:** Regularly assessing the quality and depth of digital assignments can provide insights into how effectively students are internalizing and applying what they've learned.

- **Overall Academic Performance:** Beyond individual tests and assignments, looking at overall grade point averages or end-of-term performance can provide a macro-level view of the model or tool's impact over time.

2. **Engagement Metrics:** Engagement is a cornerstone of effective learning. A student who is actively engaged is more likely to grasp and retain concepts. Thankfully, many digital platforms come equipped with built-in analytics that can help measure this.

- **Login Frequency:** If students are logging into a platform regularly, it suggests they're finding value and are engaged with the content.

- **Time Spent on Tasks:** Monitoring the time dedicated to tasks by the students can provide insights into their commitment and immersion levels.

- **Participation Rates:** Beyond just logging in, how actively are students participating? Are they contributing to discussions, collaborating on projects, or merely observing? Active participation metrics can illuminate this.

3. **Completion Rates:** Completion rates shed light on students' perseverance, understanding, and the effectiveness of the digital tool or task.

- **Digital Assignments:** Measure the number of students who see a digital assignment through to the end. This can reflect the assignment's clarity, the tool's user-friendliness, and the students' understanding of the subject.

- **Digital Projects:** Longer-term projects can often be a litmus test for sustained interest and deeper comprehension. Tracking completion rates for these can offer insights into both the effectiveness of the tool and the depth of students' understanding.

- **Courses:** For schools using digital coursework or modules, tracking the percentage of students who complete these courses (and the time they take) can provide a macro-level understanding of engagement and comprehension.

These quantitative metrics, grounded in hard data, serve as powerful tools in the educator's arsenal. They offer a snapshot of the tangible impacts of the iTECH model and other Edtech tools and guide educators towards informed decisions and continuous improvement.

Qualitative Metrics

While numbers provide tangible evidence of progress, the nuanced experiences, feelings, and perceptions that qualitative data brings are equally crucial to assessing the overall impact of the iTECH model and innovative educational technology in the classroom. This rich, descriptive data provides depth and brings forth the human element in offering a more comprehensive understanding of iTech's impact on the teaching-learning environment.

1. **Student Feedback:** Students are at the heart of the educational process, and their voices offer invaluable insights.

   - **Surveys:** Regularly administered surveys can capture students' perceptions of their learning experiences, their comfort with the digital tools, and any challenges they face.

- **Focus Groups:** Organizing small group discussions can allow for deeper dives into specific topics and yield insights that might not come up in broader surveys.

- **Individual Interviews**: One-on-one conversations with students can provide a safe space for them to share their experiences, opinions, and suggestions regarding the iTECH model and its implementation.

2. **Teacher Feedback:** Teachers are the primary drivers of the iTECH model in the classroom. Their feedback provides a first-hand account of how it integrates with teaching methodologies and its direct impact.

- **Feedback Forms:** Regular feedback forms can offer educators a platform to share their thoughts on the model's effectiveness, the tools' user-friendliness, and the support required.

- **Discussion Forums:** Organizing teacher-centric forums or meetings can foster collaborative sharing of best practices, challenges faced, and potential solutions.

- **Reflection Journals:** Encouraging teachers to maintain reflection journals can capture the evolving journey of integrating the iTECH model. They can track both successes and areas for improvement.

3. **Classroom Observations:** Direct observation provides a real-time snapshot of the classroom dynamics when the iTECH model is in action.

- **Engagement Levels:** Observe how often and how deeply students engage with the digital tools. Are they merely passive recipients, or are they actively interacting, questioning, and collaborating?

- **Collaboration Dynamics:** Monitor how students work together on digital platforms. Does the technology facilitate smoother collaboration, or are there hitches?

- **Tool Utilization:** Understand how frequently and effectively students and teachers use digital tools. Are they integrating them seamlessly into the learning process, or do they seem more like an add-on?

In essence, qualitative metrics bring to the fore the lived experiences of students and educators. They capture the intangibles, the sentiments, and the subtle shifts in the teaching-learning environment, offering a more holistic picture of the iTECH model's success.

Chapter 18
Evaluating Cross-Curricular Skills

Creativity isn't just about producing a unique piece of art; it's also about thinking differently, making connections, and innovating within constraints. Similarly, critical thinking isn't limited to solving a math problem or dissecting a piece of literature; it encompasses analyzing digital content, recognizing biases, and making informed decisions in an online realm. Problem-solving, too, has expanded beyond traditional contexts, now often involving digital tools, simulations, or collaborative platforms.

To gauge these skills genuinely and holistically, educators must lean into diverse assessment strategies that not only reflect the essence of these competencies but also mirror the digital context in which they're often employed. This demands an openness to innovation, a willingness to adapt, and a recognition of the evolving nature of learning in the 21st century.

Skill Acquisition & Transfer

In the world of education, true mastery is showcased when students can seamlessly apply skills learned within a structured classroom environment in diverse contexts. The iTECH model is designed with the primary objective of imbuing students with the "four Cs": Creativity, Critical thinking,

Collaboration, and Communication. Yet, the measure of its success lies in observing how students transfer these skills beyond digital platforms, integrating them into other subjects and everyday challenges.

1. Creativity

- Classroom Observations: Witness if students are taking innovative approaches to solve problems or express ideas, not just in tech-driven assignments but in other class tasks like essays, projects, or even class discussions.

- Project-Based Learning Assessments: Monitor projects that aren't inherently tech-focused. Are students incorporating digital tools or the innovative thought processes they've acquired through the iTECH model?

2. Critical Thinking

- Real-World Problem Solving: Pose real-world challenges to students. Evaluate their ability to dissect the issue, connect it to prior knowledge, and devise logical solutions.

- Class Debates & Discussions: During debates, monitor if students employ analytical skills to comprehend, evaluate, and construct solid arguments. They should showcase a blend of their digital and traditional learning.

3. Collaboration

- Group Assignments Across Subjects: Observe group dynamics in assignments from different subjects. Are students displaying improved team coordination, understanding of group roles, and collaborative problem-solving?

- Feedback from Peer Assessments: Encourage students to assess their peers during group tasks. Feedback can provide insights into how well students work together and value each other's input.

4. Communication

- Presentations & Public Speaking: Assess if students effectively convey their ideas, both in structure and clarity, and if they're adept at using digital tools to enhance their communication.

- Writing Tasks: Beyond digital communication, evaluate students' written tasks to understand if they've harnessed the clarity and coherence of thought advocated by the iTECH model.

Real-World Application Scenarios

Organize scenarios or events where students can apply these skills in real-world contexts, like community projects, interaction with professionals, or even school-level decision-making processes. Observe if the skills acquired through the iTECH model manifest during these events.

The success of the iTECH model is intricately tied to its long-term impact. By continually evaluating how the skills acquired translate across various scenarios, educators can measure the depth and breadth of students' learning and growth.

Evaluating Creativity

In an age where rote memorization can be outperformed by any search engine, fostering and assessing creativity in students has become paramount. While creativity can seem abstract and even elusive, educators can effectively evaluate it using well-designed tools and strategies.

Digital Storytelling Tools & Multimedia Projects

- **Platform Features:** Digital storytelling platforms, such as Adobe Express or Storybird, allow students to craft narratives using a mix of text, imagery, and sound. Multimedia projects can range from digital art portfolios to video essays.

- **Benefits:** Using these tools allows students to articulate their thoughts in diverse formats, going beyond traditional essays or reports. It captures not just the content but the unique voice and perspective of each student.

Rubrics for Creativity Assessment

When assessing creativity, it's crucial to have clear criteria. A rubric can serve as a guiding light, ensuring that assessments are both fair and comprehensive. There's a sample rubric for a multimedia project on the next page.

Using such a rubric provides students with clear expectations and allows educators to give meaningful feedback, pinpointing areas of strength and suggesting avenues for growth. When consistently applied, such strategies can play a pivotal role in nurturing and recognizing creativity in the digital age.

Evaluating Critical Thinking

In a world saturated with information, the ability to think critically is invaluable. Critical thinking is not just about acquiring knowledge but discerning its validity, analyzing its relevance, and applying it meaningfully. Digital education offers a plethora of opportunities for students to flex these intellectual muscles, and educators have the task of effectively evaluating these skills.

Criteria	Exemplary (5 Points)	Proficient (4 Points)	Developing (3 Points)	Beginning (2 Points)	Not Evident (1 Point)
Originality	Presents a fresh, unique perspective. Demonstrates innovation.	Incorporates some unique elements or interpretations.	Some evidence of personal interpretation.	Relies heavily on clichés or pre-existing ideas.	Lacks original thought or perspective.
Aesthetic	Presentation is visually compelling, with a clear sense of style and composition.	Good visual cohesion and composition.	Some inconsistencies in visual style, but generally coherent.	Visual elements feel disjointed or out of sync.	Lack of clear visual style or organization.
Innovation	Utilizes tools in new or unexpected ways. Pushes boundaries of the medium.	Shows good proficiency with tools and includes some innovative elements.	Mostly uses conventional methods, but with some innovative touches.	Lacks innovation, sticking closely to conventional uses.	Uses tools in a rudimentary way without any innovative approach.
Narrative Flow	Seamless, engaging storytelling. Every element contributes to the narrative.	Clear and coherent narrative, with minor lapses.	Some inconsistencies in the story but remains mostly clear.	Story is hard to follow or feels disjointed.	Lacks a clear narrative structure or storyline.

Analyzing Digital Content: Critical thinking begins with the skill to analyze. This involves dissecting digital content to understand its structure, purpose, and bias. Tools like Diigo allow students to annotate web content, providing insights into their analytical process.

Evaluating Validity and Relevance: In the age of misinformation, evaluating the authenticity and relevance of digital content is essential. Students should be trained to distinguish between credible sources and misleading content. Platforms that curate articles, like Newsela, adjust reading levels while providing sources, allowing students to assess content critically.

Debates & Discussion Forums: Platforms like Kialo Edu offer structured environments where students can engage in debates on contemporary issues. They can present arguments, counterarguments, and evidence, showcasing their ability to evaluate different perspectives. Similarly, forums or platforms like Moodle can be set up for class discussions where students critically analyze topics, respond to peers, and delve deeper into subjects.

Problem-Based Learning (PBL) Activities: PBL platforms, like PBLWorks, pose real-world problems for students to solve, pushing them to think critically, collaborate, and come up with innovative solutions. These platforms usually involve a blend of research, discussion, and practical application, encapsulating all facets of critical thinking.

Interpretation and Application: Critical thinking isn't just about understanding information but interpreting and applying it in varied contexts. Assignments where students must apply digital knowledge to real-world scenarios, perhaps using platforms like Wakelet to curate and present their findings, can be revealing of their interpretative skills.

Evaluating critical thinking in a digital context involves looking not just at the conclusions students reach but also at the process they went through to get there. By incorporating diverse digital tools that challenge students' thought processes, educators can create an environment ripe for developing and assessing critical thinking.

Evaluating Problem-Solving Skills

The essence of problem-solving isn't just finding a solution but understanding the problem's complexities, evaluating multiple possible solutions, and then implementing the most effective one.

Scenario-Based Assessments

Real-world Context: Design assessments that present students with real-world dilemmas or challenges that they might face in their daily lives or in their future careers. These scenarios should require the application of knowledge and skills from various subjects. For instance, presenting a challenge related to climate change could involve knowledge of science, economics, and even sociology.

Breakdown of the Problem: Observe how students dissect a problem. Are they able to identify the root cause? Can they differentiate between the main issue and the peripheral issues?

Digital Simulations: Tools like PhET Interactive Simulations or Gizmos offer science and math-related problems where students can test out different solutions in a safe environment. These tools provide instant feedback, allowing students to adjust their approach and refine their problem-solving strategies.

Virtual Reality (VR) and Augmented Reality (AR): These technologies immerse students in complex environments where they must navigate challenges. For instance, an AR history app could present students with a historical dilemma, asking them to make decisions based on their knowledge of the era.

Tracking the Problem-Solving Journey

Reflections and Journals: After completing a problem-solving task, ask students to reflect on their process. What strategies did they employ? What obstacles did they encounter, and how did they overcome them? Digital platforms like Seesaw or blogs can be used for these reflective journals.

Peer Review: Encourage students to present their problem-solving approach to their peers. This not only provides an opportunity for feedback but also exposes students to multiple methods of tackling the same problem, enhancing their own repertoire of strategies.

In the digital age, problem-solving extends beyond getting the right answer; it's about the journey, the methods used, and the ability to adapt and evolve one's approach. By integrating digital tools and scenarios into the assessment process, educators can comprehensively understand a student's problem-solving prowess.

Challenges

The digital transformation of education brings with it numerous advantages, including innovative methods for assessment. However, assessing soft skills like creativity, critical thinking, and problem-solving in the digital realm also presents its own set of challenges. Recognizing and addressing these potential pitfalls is essential to ensure that evaluations are holistic, fair, and reflective of a student's abilities.

Over-reliance on digital tools can easily sway educators by their convenience and instantaneity. However, using these tools exclusively might not capture the full range of a student's soft skills. To address this issue, it's essential to balance digital assessments with face-to-face interactions, discussions, and observations, ensuring a comprehensive view of the student's skills and capabilities.

Biases in rubrics, even when implemented digitally, can contain inherent biases that may favor certain types of learners or ways of thinking over others. To mitigate this issue, regularly review and refine rubrics involving diverse educators in the process. Ensuring that the criteria are inclusive and considering multiple ways students might demonstrate a skill is crucial for fair assessment.

The digital divide poses a significant challenge, as not every student has equal access to digital tools and resources, which might impede their ability to showcase their soft skills fully. Schools should strive to provide equal opportunities, ensuring every student can access the necessary digital tools. Additionally, assessments should account for potential tech challenges students might face, leveling the playing field for all learners.

Misunderstanding the medium is another potential issue, as some students may be more tech-savvy than others. This can lead educators to mistakenly equate a student's adeptness at using a tool with their ability in a soft skill. To prevent this, ensure that assessments focus on the content and skill demonstration, not just the flashiness of the presentation. Offering training sessions for students to familiarize themselves with the tools in advance can also help.

Feedback overload can overwhelm students, especially with digital tools offering instant and continual feedback. To prevent this, be selective and intentional about provided feedback. Prioritize quality over quantity, focusing on the most crucial points for improvement or acknowledgment, thus avoiding overwhelming students with too much information.

The potential for plagiarism is heightened by the vast digital world, where students might resort to copying or slightly modifying content found online. To counter this, use plagiarism checkers and emphasize the importance of original thought. Teaching students about digital ethics and the value of authenticity is also crucial in fostering a culture of integrity.

While digital tools offer exciting avenues for assessment, educators must be vigilant to ensure that the process remains fair, unbiased, and genuinely reflective of each student's capabilities. Addressing these challenges head-on ensures that the benefits of digital assessment far outweigh the potential pitfalls.

The objective of continuous improvement isn't merely to keep pace with technological advancements but to ensure that assessment remains a genuine reflection of student understanding and skills. In the rapidly changing landscape of digital education, educators must be proactive, reflective, and committed to evolving in the best interests of their students.

As we navigate the intricacies of evaluating skills such as creativity, critical thinking, and problem-solving, it becomes paramount to employ a multifaceted assessment lens that mirrors the complexity of the digital age.

At the core, our goal remains unaltered: to ensure every student's potential is recognized, nurtured, and accurately evaluated. To achieve this goal in today's classrooms, it's essential to intertwine the principles of traditional pedagogy with the tools and techniques of the digital age, ensuring our assessment methods are as nuanced and diverse as the skills we aim to cultivate.

Chapter 19
Measuring the Effectiveness of the iTECH Model

In the bustling environment of her fifth-grade classroom, Ms. Thompson always sought ways to engage her students and foster a deeper understanding of the curriculum. However, the rapid advancements in technology and the evolving needs of her students prompted her to re-evaluate her teaching methods. This was when she was introduced to the iTECH model, a framework designed to integrate technology seamlessly into education, promoting creativity, critical thinking, collaboration, and communication.

Initially, Ms. Thompson approached the model with a mix of curiosity and skepticism. The concept of restructuring her tried-and-tested teaching methods seemed daunting. However, the more she delved into the principles of the iTECH model, the more she realized its potential to revolutionize her classroom dynamics.

With the iTECH model as her guide, Ms. Thompson began by setting long-term goals that went beyond the standard curriculum. She aimed to not only cover academic content but also equip her students with the skills needed to thrive in a technology-driven world. Her focus shifted towards fostering digital literacy, encouraging problem-solving, and nurturing a sense of innovation among her students.

The transformation in her teaching approach was gradual but significant. In the Inspire phase, she introduced new topics using captivating multimedia resources and interactive tools. This sparked her students' curiosity and set the tone for deeper exploration. For instance, when teaching about ecosystems, she used virtual reality to transport her students to diverse habitats, allowing them to experience the subject matter firsthand.

During the Try phase, Ms. Thompson encouraged her students to independently explore new digital tools and platforms. This hands-on experience helped them develop confidence in using technology and allowed them to uncover features and functionalities on their own. She observed their interactions, taking note of common challenges and misconceptions, which she later addressed during the Expand phase.

The Expand phase became a platform for structured discussions and collaborative learning. Ms. Thompson facilitated "Tech Talks," where students shared their discoveries, taught each other new skills, and collectively solved problems. This peer-to-peer interaction not only reinforced their understanding but also built a sense of community within the classroom.

In the Create phase, students applied their knowledge and skills to produce meaningful projects. Whether it was creating digital stories, designing infographics, or developing simple apps, Ms. Thompson provided the guidance and support needed while allowing her students the creative freedom to innovate.

Finally, the Huddle phase brought everything together. Students presented their projects, received constructive feedback from their peers, and reflected on their learning journey. This phase emphasized the importance of continuous improvement and reinforced the idea that learning is an ongoing process.

Through the iTECH model, Ms. Thompson witnessed a remarkable shift in her students' engagement and enthusiasm. They were not just passive recipients of information. They were active participants in their own learning process. The integration of technology had transformed her classroom into a dynamic, interactive, and collaborative space.

As Ms. Thompson reflected on her journey with the iTECH model, she realized that the adjustments she made to her teaching were not just about incorporating technology. It was about redefining her educational goals to prepare her students for the future. The skills they developed—critical thinking, creativity, collaboration, and communication—were invaluable assets that would serve them well beyond their time in her classroom.

In essence, the iTECH model had not only enhanced her teaching but also empowered her students to become lifelong learners and innovators in an ever-changing digital world.

Adaptability & Flexibility

One of the foundational principles underpinning the iTECH model is its versatility. In an ever-evolving educational landscape where each student's needs, capacities, and learning environments can vary significantly, adaptability becomes paramount. Evaluating how effortlessly the iTECH model can mold itself to diverse educational scenarios is a crucial indicator of its effectiveness. To measure its effectiveness, we can track how the model adapts to various subjects and settings.

First, consider subject versatility. The model is interdisciplinary, allowing it to be integrated into subjects as varied as mathematics, language arts, and physical education. For example, it adapts well to creating digital art in fine arts classes and plotting graphs in math classes. It's important to monitor if students can produce subject-relevant digital content across the board, whether it's an interactive history timeline or a simulated chemical experiment.

Next, look at grade-level modifications. The iTECH model offers varied depths of engagement, from basic for younger students to intricate for older ones. Analyze how tools and tasks can be scaled according to grade levels. For instance, younger students might use a basic drawing app to depict a story, while older students might employ a more sophisticated digital storytelling platform. Engagement metrics should also be used to assess if the model keeps students consistently engaged across different grade levels, ensuring that both high schoolers and primary school students find value and engagement in the activities.

Furthermore, the iTECH model must cater to diverse learning needs. Inclusivity is key. Evaluate how the model supports students with special needs. Ensure there are tools and strategies in place, such as text-to-speech functionalities for visually impaired students or interactive simulations for those with learning disabilities. Additionally, the digital content should be culturally sensitive and relevant, integrating resources that cater to students from varied backgrounds and cultures. The model is also adaptable to different paces of learning, allowing both accelerated learners and those who need more time to proceed at their comfort level.

Gathering feedback from stakeholders is essential to gauge the model's true adaptability. Educators from various subjects and grade levels can offer insights into its adaptability in their unique contexts, while students' feedback can shed light on how well the model aligns with their diverse learning needs and preferences.

The real strength of the iTECH model lies not just in its capacity to infuse technology into education but in its malleability. Its true success is mirrored in its ability to fit like a glove, irrespective of the academic context, ensuring every student, no matter their background or learning style, reaps its benefits to the fullest.

Consistency & Longevity

Any effective educational model doesn't just impress with its initial outcomes; its true worth is gauged by how enduring and deeply ingrained it becomes in the educational process over time. As technology and educational paradigms evolve, the iTECH model should not just be a fleeting trend but should prove its resilience and adaptability over prolonged periods.

1. **Ongoing Implementation**

   - Tracking Tool Usage: Keep a record of the frequency of tool usage from the iTECH model. Are certain tools consistently being integrated into lessons year after year? Or do they see a spike in usage and then dwindle away?

   - Course Integration: Monitor the number of courses or subjects that integrate the iTECH model over time. A growing number suggests that educators find consistent value in its application across different disciplines.

2. **Evolving with Technology**

   - Updates & Revisions: The digital world is ever-evolving. Successful and lasting models ensure they adapt by regularly updating their resources, tools, and strategies.

   - Feedback Loops: Set up channels where educators can give feedback on tools or methods that might have become obsolete or suggest newer, more effective alternatives.

3. **Student Performance Over Time**

   - Long-term Metrics: Beyond immediate test scores or project grades, track metrics like student engagement, retention, or enthusiasm for subjects over multiple terms or years.

   - Alumni Feedback: Reach out to students who have left the school. Their insights on how the iTECH model prepared them for further studies or the professional world can be invaluable.

4. **Institutional Support & Training**

   - Continuous Professional Development: Provide regular training sessions for educators on the iTECH model. Consistent training indicates institutional belief in the model's long-term value.

- Resource Allocation: Monitor the budget allocated to tools, resources, or training related to the iTECH model over time. Consistent or increasing investment suggests faith in its long-term efficacy.

5. **Community and Parental Feedback:**

- Regular Surveys: Gather feedback from parents about their perception of the iTECH model's impact on their children's education over time.

- Community Involvement: Are community stakeholders consistently engaged in events, workshops, or discussions around the iTECH model?

The iTECH model's true success will be demonstrated by its sustained presence, adaptability, and consistent positive impact on students. It's not just about riding the wave of innovation but also becoming a steadfast beacon guiding the educational journey for years to come.

Professional Development & Support

In the journey of implementing the iTECH model, educators are central to driving the change. Their confidence, expertise, and understanding of the model can significantly influence its success. Thus, ensuring robust professional development and support structures is pivotal. Evaluating these mechanisms is crucial to ensuring educators are equipped, supported, and motivated to integrate the iTECH model effectively.

1. **Depth & Breadth of Training**

- Training Modules: What kind of training sessions are available? Are they comprehensive, covering both foundational aspects of the iTECH model and more nuanced, advanced topics?

- Diverse Learning Opportunities: Are training programs diversified to cater to different learning styles? For instance, do they offer hands-on workshops, webinars, self-paced online modules, or mentoring sessions?

2. Accessibility & Frequency

- Regular Schedules: How often are professional development sessions held? Regularity suggests a sustained commitment to educator growth and adaptation to the evolving needs of the digital age.

- Flexibility: Are there options for educators with varying schedules, such as weekend or evening sessions or on-demand resources?

3. Feedback & Iteration

- Post-Training Surveys: After each training session, gather feedback from educators on its effectiveness, relevance, and areas of improvement.

- Adaptation: How quickly and effectively are training modules updated based on feedback and changing technological landscapes?

4. Peer-to-Peer Learning

- Collaborative Platforms: Platforms that allow educators to share experiences, resources, and insights about the iTECH model can foster a supportive community.

- Mentorship Programs: Pairing less experienced educators with seasoned ones can ensure hands-on guidance and quicker resolutions to challenges.

5. Resource Availability

- Resource Hub: Is there a centralized digital hub where educators can access tools, lesson plans, best practices, and other resources related to the iTECH model?

- Support Channels: Are there dedicated helplines or support channels where educators can seek assistance for specific challenges or queries they encounter?

6. Continuous Learning Culture

- Advanced Workshops: Beyond initial training, are there avenues for educators to dive deeper, explore advanced tools, or discuss pedagogical strategies?

- Recognition and Incentives: Recognizing and rewarding educators who actively engage with and excel in implementing the iTECH model can foster motivation and commitment.

7. Stakeholder Engagement

- Parent-Teacher Collaboration: Are there sessions or workshops that involve parents, ensuring they're aligned with the school's digital vision and can support learning at home?

- Inter-Departmental Workshops: Encourage departments to share their experiences, challenges, and best practices, ensuring a cohesive adoption of the model across subjects.

Empowering educators is foundational to the success of the iTECH model. As the adage goes, "Give a teacher the right tools, and they'll pave the way for learners' success." By ensuring robust professional development and continuous support, we're not only bolstering the iTECH model's implementation but also enriching the entire educational ecosystem.

Community & Parental Feedback

The school ecosystem extends beyond its walls, directly impacting families and the broader community. While educators have a firsthand view of the iTECH model's classroom implications, parents and guardians observe its residual and long-term effects on students at home. Their feedback provides invaluable insights, ensuring that the model's influence transcends the classroom, becoming ingrained in the student's everyday life.

1. **Parent-Teacher Meetings**

   - Regular Check-ins: Establishing periodic meetings specifically to discuss the iTECH model's influence can shed light on a child's enthusiasm, understanding, and any possible reservations about technology use.

   - Open Forums: Hosting sessions where parents can openly discuss their observations, concerns, and suggestions related to the model can foster a sense of community involvement and partnership.

2. **Surveys & Feedback Forms**

   - Digital Platforms: Using tools like Google Forms or SurveyMonkey to create detailed surveys allows parents to anonymously share their thoughts, offering genuine feedback about the model's impact.

   - Feedback Analysis: Regularly analyze this feedback, categorizing it to discern patterns, common concerns, or widespread appreciation.

3. **Digital Show & Tell:**

   - Student-led Demonstrations: Organize events where students showcase what they've achieved using the iTECH model to their parents. This boosts student confidence and provides parents with a firsthand view of its benefits.

- Parental Involvement: Encourage parents to engage in these sessions, ask questions, and share their observations.

4. Community Workshops

- Digital Literacy for Parents: Hosting workshops that echo the themes of the iTECH model can bridge any generational tech gaps, empowering parents to understand and appreciate their child's digital learning journey better.

- Feedback Channels: Ensure these workshops have segments where parents can voice their observations, concerns, or suggestions.

5. Collaboration with Parent-Teacher Associations (PTAs)

- Regular Updates: Engage with PTAs, offering regular updates about the model's progress, adaptations, and outcomes.

- Feedback Mechanisms: PTAs can be instrumental in gathering broader community feedback, especially from parents who might be less vocal individually.

6. Digital Portfolios for Parents

- Showcase Progress: Platforms where students can compile and showcase their work can be shared with parents, allowing them to directly see the results of the iTECH model's implementation.

- Commenting and Interaction: Enabling features where parents can comment or interact with these portfolios can serve as a continuous feedback loop.

- Incorporating feedback from the community, especially parents, ensures that the iTECH model is not just a classroom strategy, but a holistic approach to education. This wider perspective ensures that any adjustments made to the model consider both classroom realities and the broader implications of digital learning in a student's life.

Cost-Benefit Analysis

While budgets are essential, the real value lies in the impact on student learning, teacher efficacy, and overall school performance. For administrators, it's vital to strike a balance, ensuring that financial outlays for technology and training translate into tangible academic and holistic benefits.

1. **Financial Investment**

   - Technology Infrastructure: The initial outlay for devices, software licenses, and digital platforms can be substantial. It's essential to consider not just the upfront costs but also maintenance, upgrades, and potential replacements.

   - Training & Professional Development: Implementing the iTECH model isn't just about having the right tools. Investing in teacher training ensures that the technology is used effectively and pedagogically.

2. **Academic Returns**

   - Student Performance: Track metrics such as test scores, project grades, and overall academic improvements. While direct correlations might be challenging to pinpoint, a general upward trend can indicate a positive Return on Investment (ROI).

   - Engagement & Participation: Beyond grades, increased student engagement, participation, and enthusiasm can be invaluable indicators of the model's success.

3. **Holistic Benefits**

   - Skill Development: Assess the enhancement in 'soft' skills such as critical thinking, creativity, collaboration, and communication. While harder to quantify, these skills are crucial for students' future readiness.

- Teacher Efficiency: With the right tools and training, teachers might find they can achieve better results in less time or with less repetitive effort. This increased efficiency can be a significant return on investment.

4. Long-Term Impacts

- Future Readiness: While immediate academic benefits are essential, the long-term impact of preparing students for a digital future should not be underestimated in the cost-benefit equation.

- Tech Sustainability: Consider the longevity and adaptability of tech investments. Platforms and tools that can evolve with educational needs offer better long-term value.

5. Comparative Analysis

- Alternative Models: Compare the iTECH model's outcomes against other educational strategies or previous methodologies employed in the institution. This comparison can offer a clearer picture of the value derived from investments.

- Benchmarking: If possible, compare the performance with similar schools or institutions that haven't adopted the iTECH model.

6. Intangible Returns

- School Reputation: Enhanced academic outcomes and modern teaching methodologies can bolster a school's reputation, making it more appealing to potential parents and students.

- Community Engagement: A robust digital education model can foster stronger ties with the community, leading to potential partnerships, sponsorships, or other collaborative ventures.

While the immediate costs of implementing the iTECH model might be apparent, the benefits—both tangible and intangible—must be assessed over a more extended period. For administrators, this cost-benefit analysis provides a holistic view, ensuring that investments today yield fruitful results for tomorrow's learners.

The iTECH model's success hinges on its adaptability and commitment to continuous refinement. By proactively tracking its effectiveness and staying open to changes, schools can ensure that the model remains a potent force that empowers students in the digital age.

Commitment to Evolution in Technology-Rich Learning

The digital landscape of education is fluid, constantly reshaped by technological innovations and evolving pedagogical practices. This dynamic nature calls for an equally dynamic approach to implement technology-rich learning experiences. It's not enough to simply introduce digital tools and methodologies into the classroom. The real challenge—and opportunity—lies in the continuous reflection and refinement of these implementations.

Reflection is the cornerstone of any meaningful educational endeavor. By periodically stepping back and examining the efficacy, reach, and outcomes of our digital initiatives, educators can identify both successes and challenges. Such reflective practices pave the way for targeted improvements and ensures that technology integration is always aligned with the ultimate goal: enhancing student learning and holistic development.

Moreover, in a world where technology's pace is often dizzying, staying updated is non-negotiable. New tools, platforms, and digital strategies emerge frequently. While it's impractical (and unnecessary) to adopt every new trend, it's crucial to be discerning, identifying those innovations that can genuinely elevate the learning experience.

Collaboration remains key in this journey of continuous improvement.

Sharing experiences, successes, challenges, and insights among educators creates a rich tapestry of knowledge. From formal professional development sessions to informal teacher lounge discussions, every interaction offers a potential for learning.

However, perhaps the most potent feedback comes directly from the classroom's heart—the students. Their experiences, feedback, and outcomes are the most authentic indicators of whether our digital endeavors are hitting the mark. By creating avenues for student feedback and genuinely considering their inputs, educators can craft technology-rich experiences that resonate deeply and meaningfully.

Finally, as we advocate for technology's integration into education, let's remember its role: a tool, a facilitator. The heart of education remains the human connection—the rapport between teacher and student, the joy of discovery, the thrill of overcoming challenges. Technology should augment these experiences, not replace them.

While the integration of technology in education offers unprecedented opportunities for enriched learning, its real power lies in its thoughtful, reflective, and continuous application. As educators, we must be committed to perpetual evolution, always striving for the ideal intersection of technology and pedagogy that best serves our students.

Chapter 20
Professional Development

Teaching in the digital age requires an ongoing commitment to professional growth. As technology evolves at a breakneck pace, educators must remain agile, continually updating their skill sets. Moreover, collaboration among educators can lead to a richer, more holistic integration of the iTECH model across subjects and grade levels.

Ms. Anderson's journey to discovering the iTECH model began at a mid-year professional development workshop hosted by her school district. Always eager to find new ways to engage her students, she approached the day with an open mind, hoping to glean some fresh ideas to bring back to her classroom. Little did she know the workshop would completely transform her teaching approach.

As she entered the workshop, Ms. Anderson noticed a buzz of excitement among her fellow educators. The agenda highlighted a new instructional model by Brittany Washburn (the author of this book) designed to integrate technology seamlessly into the classroom, fostering creativity, critical thinking, and collaboration among students. The presenter, Mr. Jensen, a seasoned educator with a knack for technology integration, began with an overview of the iTECH model. He emphasized how it was not just about using digital tools but about creating a dynamic learning environment where technology enhances and enriches the learning experience.

Mr. Jensen's enthusiasm was contagious. He demonstrated how the iTECH model could be applied across various subjects and grade levels, using real-life examples from his own classroom. He showcased student projects that ranged from digital storytelling in language arts to virtual science experiments and even math simulations that made abstract concepts tangible. Each example illustrated how the iTECH model's phases—Inspire, Try, Expand, Create, and Huddle—worked together to create a cohesive and engaging learning experience.

Intrigued by the potential of the iTECH model, Ms. Anderson attended breakout sessions that delved deeper into each phase. During the Inspire session, she learned how to capture a class' attention with compelling digital content. The Try session provided a hands-on experience with new educational apps and tools which encouraged educators to let students explore and discover independently. In the Expand session, she saw the value of structured discussions where students shared their discoveries and misconceptions were addressed. The Create session inspired her with ideas for student projects that combined creativity with critical thinking. Finally, the Huddle session emphasized the importance of peer feedback and reflection.

As the day progressed, Ms. Anderson's initial skepticism turned into excitement. She realized that the iTECH model could help her create a more interactive and student-centered classroom. She was particularly impressed by how the model encouraged students to take ownership of their learning and collaborate with their peers. The practical tips and strategies shared by Mr. Jensen gave her the confidence to try the iTECH model in her own classroom.

By the end of the workshop, Ms. Anderson felt invigorated and ready to implement what she had learned. She spent the weekend planning her first iTECH lesson, eager to see how her students would respond. When Monday morning arrived, she introduced her class to the digital storytelling tool they would use following the steps she had learned in the workshop.

The transformation was immediate. Her students were captivated by the Inspire phase, where she showcased an animated video. During the Try phase, they eagerly explored the storytelling tool, discovering its features and capabilities. The Expand phase brought lively discussions and shared insights, while the Create phase saw students producing imaginative digital stories. The Huddle phase provided valuable feedback and reflection, helping students refine their work and learn from each other.

Seeing the excitement and engagement in her classroom, Ms. Anderson knew she had found a powerful tool in the iTECH model. She continued to refine her approach, share her successes and challenges with her colleagues, and contribute to a growing community of educators committed to transforming education through technology.

The Imperative of Continuous Learning for Educators

The tools and platforms available for education are continually evolving, offering new possibilities for instruction. Staying updated ensures teachers can maximize these tools for student engagement and learning.

As we learn more about how students engage with technology, instructional strategies must adjust. Continuous professional development ensures that educators are equipped with the latest effective methodologies. Teachers confident in their technological prowess can instill a similar confidence in their students. They can model the curiosity and adaptability vital in our digital era.

Championing Interdepartmental Collaboration

Interdepartmental collaboration can contribute to the success of the iTECH model. To promote this collaboration, organize regular sessions where educators from different departments share how they've integrated technology. This can lead to innovative, cross-curricular project ideas.

Create a centralized digital repository where teachers can contribute and access lesson plans, tools, or ideas related to the iTECH model. Encourage educators to observe their peers, especially those adept at integrating technology. Such observations can offer practical insights and foster a culture of shared learning.

Promote projects where two or more subjects integrate, utilizing technology. For instance, a history lesson can merge with a digital arts class to create multimedia presentations on historical periods. After collaborative projects or shared sessions, create avenues for feedback. This can help in refining the approach, tools, or strategies used.

For the iTECH model to be seamlessly integrated into the curriculum, educators must also be learners. They must embrace new tools, strategies, and collaborations. By investing in professional development and fostering a collaborative teaching environment, schools can ensure that the iTECH model is holistically implemented, benefiting every student.

Continual Learning: The Changing Digital Landscape

Each day, we encounter new apps, platforms, threats, and opportunities. With the landscape evolving at a breakneck speed, our understanding and approach to digital citizenship and online safety must be dynamic. We must always be catching up or staying ahead.

While many of us may reminisce about the early days of the internet—a simpler time dominated by web browsers and emails—today's youth are navigating a far more intricate web. They're dealing with an entire ecosystem: from social media platforms to augmented reality games and from deepfakes to virtual classrooms. What was considered best practice even a couple of years ago may now be outdated.

Therefore, continual learning is necessary. Given the fluidity of the digital world, a one-time lesson or workshop on digital citizenship isn't sufficient. We must treat our knowledge of the online realm similarly to how we treat software: in need of regular updates. The digital world constantly offers innovative tools for learning, creativity, and connection. Being updated means we can harness these opportunities for our benefit and the benefit of our students.

As technology becomes more intelligent, so do potential threats. Phishing tactics, cyberbullying techniques, and scam strategies evolve. By continually learning, we ensure we're not caught off guard.

Strategies for Continual Learning:

1. **Regular Training:** Schools and institutions should prioritize regular training sessions for teachers, students, and parents. These sessions can address new tools, emerging threats, and altered digital behaviors.

2. **Engage in Online Communities:** There are numerous online forums, webinars, and communities where educators, parents, and tech experts discuss the latest in the digital realm. This can provide real-time insights.

3. **Subscribe to Newsletters and Blogs:** There are several organizations, like Common Sense Media or Cyberwise, that provide regular updates about the digital world's changing dynamics.

4. **Feedback Loop:** Encourage students and educators to share their online experiences. Sometimes, they're the first to encounter a new app or a fresh challenge. Creating an environment where they can share ensures the community learns collectively.

5. **Dedicated Digital Citizenship Curriculum Review:** Just as academic curricula undergoes reviews and updates, so should the digital citizenship curriculum. This ensures it remains relevant and effective.

Our journey through the digital world is akin to sailing in ever-changing waters. While we can't predict every wave or challenge, we can ensure our ship—our knowledge of digital citizenship—is always in top shape, ready to face whatever comes its way. Continual learning isn't just a strategy; in today's world, it's a necessity.

Chapter 21
Challenges and Solutions

While the iTECH model holds tremendous promise for revolutionizing classroom instruction and deepening student engagement, its integration is not without potential challenges. Recognizing and addressing these challenges head-on can enhance the transition's efficacy.

Ms. Anderson's colleague, Mrs. Harris, had always been an exceptional teacher. With over twenty years of experience, she had developed a strong rapport with her students and a knack for delivering engaging lessons. However, when the school district introduced the iTECH model, Mrs. Harris felt a pang of resistance. The idea of integrating so much technology into her classroom seemed overwhelming, and she was uncertain how it would fit into her established teaching methods.

The first hurdle Mrs. Harris faced was information overload. The professional development sessions provided a wealth of information about various digital tools and the iTECH model's phases. Despite her best efforts to keep up, Mrs. Harris felt bombarded with too many new concepts at once. She struggled to see how she could seamlessly incorporate these tools into her lessons without disrupting the flow she had perfected over the years.

Adding to her apprehension were the limitations of her classroom's technology infrastructure. The school's internet was often slow and unreliable, and the number of available devices was insufficient for her large class sizes. Mrs. Harris worried about the logistical challenges of implementing the iTECH model, such as ensuring every student had access to the necessary technology and troubleshooting technical issues during lessons.

Moreover, Mrs. Harris had concerns about student disengagement. She had witnessed firsthand how easily students could become distracted by technology. The thought of incorporating more digital tools into her classroom made her anxious that students would focus more on the gadgets than the learning objectives. She feared losing the personal connection she had with her students, which she believed was crucial for their academic success.

Despite these concerns, Mrs. Harris decided to give the iTECH model a try. She started with a simple project, introducing her students to a digital storytelling app. However, the challenges she feared quickly materialized. The internet connection lagged, causing frustration among students who were eager to explore the app. Some students struggled to navigate the tool, leading to many raised hands and requests for help. Mrs. Harris found herself bouncing between students, trying to resolve technical issues rather than facilitating learning.

Feeling overwhelmed, Mrs. Harris reverted to her traditional teaching methods, convinced that the iTECH model was unsuitable for her classroom. During a lunch break, she confided in Ms. Anderson, expressing her frustrations and doubts. "I just don't see how this technology can work for me," she admitted. "It's too much to handle, and my students aren't engaged. They just see it as playtime."

Ms. Anderson listened empathetically. She had faced her own challenges when first implementing the iTECH model but persevered and found a way to make it work. "I understand how you feel," she said gently. "It took me a while to get comfortable with it, too. Maybe we can work together to find a way to integrate it that feels manageable for you."

With Ms. Anderson's support, Mrs. Harris decided to give the iTECH model another shot, but this time with a more structured approach. They started by addressing the technology infrastructure issues, working with the school's IT department to ensure a more reliable internet connection and securing additional devices. Ms. Anderson also suggested starting with the basics, focusing on one digital tool at a time and gradually building up Mrs. Harris's confidence.

Together, they planned a lesson using the iTECH model's phases but kept it simple and achievable. For the Inspire phase, they used a short, engaging video related to the lesson topic. During the Try phase, they allowed students to explore a basic digital tool with clear instructions and a set time limit. The Expand phase involved a structured discussion where students shared their discoveries, and Mrs. Harris addressed any misconceptions. For the Create phase, they chose a straightforward project that required students to apply their learning creatively but didn't rely heavily on advanced tech skills. Finally, in the Huddle phase, students presented their work and received constructive feedback from peers.

Over time, Mrs. Harris began to see the benefits of the iTECH model. Her initial fears about student disengagement diminished as she observed her students' excitement and creativity. She realized that by taking a gradual approach and leveraging the support of her colleagues, she could effectively integrate technology without feeling overwhelmed. The experience taught her the importance of adaptability and the value of embracing new methods to enhance student learning.

Resistance to Change from Educators

Some educators, particularly those who have been teaching for many years, might resist or be skeptical about incorporating technology or adopting new instructional models. Here are some strategies to address this:

1. **Targeted Professional Development:** Tailor training sessions to meet the varied tech proficiency levels of staff. Offering beginner, intermediate, and advanced workshops can help.

2. **Mentorship Programs:** Pair tech-savvy educators with those less comfortable with technology. This peer mentorship can offer hands-on support and model successful integration.

3. **Success Stories:** Showcase tangible benefits by sharing success stories or case studies where the iTECH model has made a significant difference in student outcomes.

Technology Infrastructure Limitations

Not all schools have the same access to technology resources, which can limit the application of the iTECH model. This disparity is especially problematic in low-income areas, where funding for technology is often insufficient. Schools in these regions may struggle with outdated equipment, lack of internet access, or insufficient digital tools, further widening the educational gap.

Addressing the lack of technology can be approached through several strategies:

1. **Grants and Funding**: Seek out grants specifically designed for educational technology enhancement. Organizations like ISTE and EdTechTeam often provide or highlight funding opportunities.

2. **Bring Your Own Device (BYOD) Policy**: Encourage students to use their personal devices, ensuring necessary precautions are in place to maintain cyber safety.

3. **Open-Source Tools**: Utilize free and open-source educational tools available online, maximizing resources without straining the budget.

By implementing these solutions, schools can work towards bridging the digital divide and ensuring all students can access the technology they need to succeed.

Overwhelm and Information Overload

With the vast array of digital tools available, educators might feel overwhelmed about which to use and how to integrate them effectively. Here are some ideas to prevent this:

1. **Curated Tool Lists:** Create a recommended list of vetted tools for various subjects and grade levels. Update this list regularly.

2. **Step-by-Step Integration:** Recommend teachers to start small, incorporating one tool at a time until they gain confidence.

3. **Continuous Training:** Offer refreshers and new training sessions throughout the academic year, ensuring educators feel supported.

Student Resistance or Disengagement:

Not all students may immediately see the benefits of the iTECH model, especially if they are more used to traditional teaching methods. Here are some best practices to fully engage students with the model:

1. **Student Choice:** Allow students to choose between various tools or platforms, giving them a sense of ownership in their learning.

2. **Real-World Relevance:** Align projects and tasks with real-world applications, so students see the direct relevance and importance of their work.

3. **Feedback Loops:** Regularly solicit feedback from students, making adjustments based on their experiences and preferences.

Concerns About Screen Time and Digital Distractions

With increased use of technology, concerns about excessive screen time or digital distractions might arise. Here are some ways to address this.

1. **Balanced Integration:** Ensure that the iTECH model is part of a balanced instructional approach, incorporating offline activities and hands-on projects.

2. **Digital Etiquette and Citizenship:** Incorporate lessons on responsible technology use, teaching students about the importance of breaks and focusing on tasks.

While the iTECH model's integration presents challenges, these hurdles can be overcome with proactive strategies and a commitment to continuous learning and adjustment. By focusing on the end goal – enhanced student engagement and improved learning outcomes – educators can navigate the path to successful technology integration with clarity and confidence.

Education must rise to meet the challenges and opportunities that new technologies present. The iTECH model isn't just a framework for integrating technology into the classroom—it's a comprehensive approach to shaping the future of education, one that prepares students for the dynamic digital world that lies ahead.

Educators, too, stand to gain immensely. By embracing the iTECH model, they're not just updating their teaching methods. They're pioneering a movement that redefines the classroom's boundaries. They become facilitators of dynamic, engaging learning environments where students are empowered to explore, innovate, and drive their own learning experiences.

As we reflect on the journey of integrating the iTECH model across the curriculum, it's essential to acknowledge that technology in education is not an end in itself. It is a means to a much greater end: shaping learners who are ready to face the challenges of the future, who can adapt to the ever-evolving digital landscape, and who can leverage technology to make meaningful contributions to the world.

The future belongs to those who can harness the power of technology to imagine and actualize new possibilities. Through the iTECH model, we nurture a generation of students who will be at the forefront of this revolution. They will be ready to lead with creativity, critical thinking, and a collaborative spirit.

Section 5
Ethics of Technology

Chapter 22
What is Digital Citizenship?

The ways in which we interact, communicate, learn, and entertain have shifted profoundly. Amidst this transformation, the concept of digital citizenship has emerged as a crucial framework. So, what does it entail?

Digital citizenship, at its core, refers to the responsible and effective use of technology, particularly within an online environment. It doesn't merely revolve around being online but emphasizes the quality, ethics, and impact of our digital interactions. It encapsulates everything from understanding the nuances of online etiquette and respecting intellectual property rights to safeguarding one's privacy and standing against cyberbullying.

Ms. Turner, a seasoned middle-school teacher, understands the importance of digital citizenship, online safety, digital literacy, and the ethical use of technology in her classroom. She believes these skills are crucial for preparing her students to navigate the digital world responsibly and effectively.

To develop these skills, Ms. Turner integrates a comprehensive digital literacy curriculum into her lessons. She starts by introducing her students to the concept of digital citizenship. It involves teaching them about their rights and responsibilities when using technology. This includes understanding privacy, respecting intellectual property, and recognizing the impact of their digital footprint.

For online safety, Ms. Turner uses interactive activities to educate her students about the potential risks of the internet. She discusses topics like cyberbullying, phishing scams, and protecting personal information. She often uses real-world examples and scenarios to make these lessons relatable and impactful.

In her digital literacy lessons, Ms. Turner focuses on teaching her students how to critically evaluate online information. She introduces them to various tools and strategies for assessing the credibility of sources, understanding bias, and distinguishing between reliable and unreliable content. This helps her students become discerning consumers of digital information.

To emphasize the ethical use of technology, Ms. Turner incorporates discussions and projects that explore the ethical implications of digital actions. She encourages her students to think about the consequences of plagiarism, the importance of citing sources, and the ethical considerations of social media use. Through these activities, her students learn to make thoughtful and ethical decisions in their digital interactions.

Throughout the school year, Ms. Turner uses a variety of digital tools and platforms to reinforce these concepts. For example, she uses classroom blogs for students to practice respectful and constructive online communication. She also leverages educational apps that simulate real-life digital dilemmas, allowing students to apply their knowledge in a safe and controlled environment.

By actively incorporating digital citizenship, online safety, digital literacy, and ethical use of technology into her teaching, Ms. Turner equips her students with the skills they need to navigate the digital world confidently and responsibly. Her proactive approach enhances their academic experience and prepares them for the challenges and opportunities of the digital age.

The Significance of Practicing Responsible Digital Behavior

Understanding and embodying responsible digital behavior is paramount for several reasons:

1. **Safety:** The online realm, while offering a plethora of opportunities, also poses risks—cyberbullying, scams, misinformation, to name a few. Being a responsible digital citizen means being equipped to navigate these challenges safely.

2. **Reputation:** Our digital footprints, consisting of our likes, shares, comments, uploads, and more, are enduring. In many ways, they define our digital identity. Practicing responsible online behavior helps build a positive digital reputation that can influence real-world consequences, be it in friendships, academic endeavors, or job opportunities.

3. **Empathy:** Just as in the physical world, our actions in the digital sphere impact others. Responsible digital behavior underscores the significance of understanding and respecting the feelings and rights of others, promoting a more inclusive and harmonious online community.

4. **Legal Implications:** Several online actions, such as piracy or spreading defamatory content, can have legal consequences. Being a diligent digital citizen means being aware of these boundaries and respecting the law.

5. **Empowerment:** Proper digital citizenship isn't just about defense—it's also about offense. It empowers users to leverage the internet's vast potential positively, be it for learning, activism, entrepreneurship, or creativity.

Digital citizenship isn't a mere buzzword—it's a compass that guides our journey in the digital universe. By understanding and practicing responsible digital behavior, we not only protect and empower ourselves but also contribute to a healthier, more constructive digital community.

Key Elements of Digital Citizenship

In the sprawling landscape of the digital world, navigating safely and responsibly requires a multi-faceted understanding. The intricacies of digital citizenship are vast, but for educators and students alike, grasping some core elements is pivotal. Here, we will delve into three critical pillars: digital literacy, digital etiquette, and digital law.

1. **Digital Literacy:** Digital literacy goes beyond the basic ability to use digital tools; it's about the proficiency to harness them effectively and responsibly.

   • Finding Information: In the age of information overflow, the capability to locate relevant and trustworthy content is crucial. This involves knowing which sources are credible and discerning fact from fiction.

   • Evaluating Content: Not all online content is created equal. Digital literacy means having the critical thinking skills to assess the quality, reliability, and value of what one encounters online.

   • Creating and Communicating: Digital literacy also encompasses the ability to create digital content, be it through writing, video production, or other mediums. Furthermore, it's about communicating this content in a clear, effective, and respectful manner.

2. **Digital Etiquette:** Much like the real world, the digital sphere has its own set of unspoken norms and expected behaviors. Together, these

things form the essence of digital etiquette.

- Respectful Interactions: Just because online interactions provide a veil of anonymity doesn't mean respect gets tossed out the window. Being kind, not engaging in or endorsing cyberbullying, and understanding the impact of one's words are fundamental.

- Privacy Matters: Part of digital etiquette is understanding what to share and what to withhold. This includes not sharing others' private information or photos without permission.

- Acknowledging and Crediting: When sharing or utilizing someone else's content, it's courteous (and often required) to give credit. This can be as simple as tagging the original creator or linking back to the source.

3. **Digital Law:** The digital world, while seemingly boundless, is governed by a set of laws and regulations designed to maintain order, protect rights, and ensure safety.

- Copyright: This is a form of protection given to creators of original works of authorship, whether they are literary, artistic, musical, or certain other intellectual works. Downloading, reproducing, or distributing copyrighted content without permission is illegal.

- Fair Use: While copyright laws protect creators, the principle of fair use allows limited use of copyrighted material without permission for purposes like criticism, comment, news reporting, teaching, scholarship, or research.

- Privacy Laws: With the digital age came concerns about how personal data was collected, stored, and used. Various laws and regulations are in place to protect individual privacy online.

Understanding these elements and integrating them into one's digital life is crucial. They serve as the foundational pillars upon which a responsible, informed, and effective digital citizenship is built.

It's often said that the internet is written in ink, not pencil. Deleted videos, photos, or posts can be archived, screenshotted, or stored in caches. Data, once out there, never truly disappears. This permanence means that past actions can impact future opportunities, relationships, and one's personal and professional reputation.

In essence, the digital realm is not a separate universe. It's closely interwoven with our everyday lives. Recognizing this connection and the potential consequences of online actions is the first step toward responsible digital citizenship. The stories above aren't just cautionary tales; they're reminders that in the age of the internet, our actions, both online and offline, define us in ways we might not always anticipate.

Chapter 23
Online Safety

Technology permeates every facet of our daily lives. Online safety isn't just a feature. It's a necessity. With the increasing number of users, especially young learners navigating the digital space, the risks have magnified. However, with the right knowledge and tools, these pitfalls can be substantially mitigated. Here's a closer look at how students can shield themselves from potential online hazards:

1. **Personal Information Protection:** A golden rule of the digital world is to treat personal information like gold—valuable and not to be casually shared.

   • Limit Sharing: Students should be educated to avoid disclosing personal details, such as their full name, address, phone number, school name, and their friends' and family members' details. This safeguards them from potential predators and identity thieves.

   • Think Before Posting: Social media can make sharing seem innocuous. However, students should be taught that once something is online, it might stay there forever even if deleted. They should be cautious about posting photos or information that can reveal their location or daily routines.

2. Recognizing and Avoiding Online Threats:

- Phishing Scams: These are fraudulent attempts to obtain sensitive information, often through deceptive emails or messages. Students should be taught to distrust unsolicited communications and to not click on suspicious links.

- Malware: Malicious software can harm or exploit any device. Students should learn the importance of not downloading files or apps from untrusted sources.

- Cyberbullying: Students should be taught to recognize the signs of cyberbullying, both as potential victims and bystanders. They should be encouraged to report any bullying they experience or witness and to support peers who are targeted.

3. Proper Password Practices:

- Strong Passwords: A good password is like a strong lock. Students should be educated about creating complex passwords that use a mix of letters, numbers, and symbols. They should avoid using easily guessable information, like birthdays or names.

- Keep Passwords Private: Sharing might be caring but not with passwords. Students should understand the importance of keeping their passwords confidential to prevent unauthorized access to their accounts.

4. Secure Browsing:

- Recognizing HTTPS: Students should be taught to identify websites with "HTTPS" in their URLs, indicating they are secure. These sites encrypt data which makes it harder for hackers to intercept information.

- Avoid Public Wi-Fi for Sensitive Tasks: Public networks are often less secure. Students should avoid activities like online shopping or checking bank accounts when connected to public Wi-Fi.

To thrive in the digital age, students don't just need to be tech-savvy; they need to be tech-safe. By instilling these principles early on, we equip them with the shields they need to navigate the vast digital world confidently and securely.

Chapter 24
Digital Literacy

In the tapestry of contemporary education, one thread is becoming increasingly pronounced: digital literacy. No longer a supplementary skill, digital literacy has become a cornerstone of modern education, integral to preparing students for the complexities of the 21st century.

In an age where digital technology permeates almost every aspect of our lives, the ability to effectively navigate, understand, and utilize this technology is crucial. Digital literacy extends beyond the basic ability to use software or operate a device; it involves a deeper understanding of how technology works, how it impacts society, and how it can be used responsibly.

Educational curricula worldwide are increasingly incorporating digital literacy to ensure students are not just passive consumers of digital content but are also savvy creators and critical thinkers. This shift recognizes that digital literacy is no longer a luxury but a necessity for academic success, career readiness, and informed citizenship.

Equipping Students with Essential 21st-Century Skills

1. **Critical Thinking and Problem-Solving:** Digital literacy encourages students to think critically about the information they encounter

online. It involves evaluating the credibility of sources, understanding the biases in digital content, and making informed decisions based on this analysis.

2. **Creativity and Innovation:** With digital tools at their fingertips, students have unprecedented opportunities to create and innovate. Whether it's designing a digital art piece, coding a new app, or producing a multimedia presentation, digital literacy unleashes a student's creative potential.

3. **Communication and Collaboration:** The digital world offers myriad platforms for communication and collaboration, transcending geographical boundaries. Digital literacy equips students with the skills to effectively collaborate in this global digital landscape, preparing them for a workforce that is increasingly remote and interconnected.

4. **Digital Citizenship:** Understanding the ethical use of technology, respecting intellectual property, and engaging positively in online communities are all facets of digital literacy. This aspect prepares students to be responsible members of the digital world.

5. **Adaptability and Lifelong Learning:** In a world where technological change is the only constant, digital literacy fosters adaptability and a mindset geared towards lifelong learning. It prepares students not just for the technologies of today but for the agility to embrace the technologies of tomorrow.

As we forge ahead in the 21st century, the integration of digital literacy into education is not just a trend. It's a fundamental shift in how we prepare students for the future. By embedding digital literacy in the educational curriculum, we are equipping students with a toolkit of skills essential for success in a rapidly evolving digital world.

Chapter 25
Ethical Use of Technology

Sarah, a high school blogger, used an image she found online for one of her blog posts, thinking that everything online was "free to use." A few months later, she received a hefty fine for copyright infringement. Digital laws, including those about copyright, are very much enforceable. Ignorance of these rules isn't an excuse in the eyes of the law.

Understanding the ethical considerations tied to technology use is pivotal. Just as we expect ethical behavior in face-to-face interactions, the digital sphere demands its own set of moral standards. Let's delve into the pivotal areas of ethical technology use.

1. Plagiarism and Copyright

- Valuing Original Work: With the vast array of information and content available online, it's easy to copy and paste without giving it a second thought. However, students should be taught that every piece of content—from articles to images—has someone's effort behind it. Using someone else's work without permission or credit is illegal.

- Citing Properly: Recognizing the value of original content means understanding how to give credit where it's due. This involves teaching students how to properly cite sources, whether they're quoting a statement or using an image.

- Seeking Permission: If students wish to use copyrighted content, they should learn to seek permission or look for content that's available for reuse, such as those under Creative Commons licenses.

2. Netiquette

- Mindful Interaction: Just as we follow decorum in physical settings, the online world has its own etiquette. This involves being respectful in discussions, avoiding ALL CAPS (which can come across as shouting), and being empathetic toward others' viewpoints.

- Avoiding Trolling and Cyberbullying: Engaging in aggressive behavior, baiting, or intentionally upsetting others is a strict no. Students should understand the emotional toll such actions can have and be taught to behave online as they would in person.

- Mindful Sharing: Before sharing or forwarding any piece of information, it's crucial to verify its authenticity. Spreading false or misleading information, even unintentionally, can have far-reaching consequences.

3. Digital Footprint

- Lasting Online Imprints: Every click, like, share, comment, or upload contributes to one's digital footprint. Students should be made aware that, in many cases, this footprint is permanent. Even deleted content can often be retrieved or might have been screen-shot and shared by others.

- Thinking Before Posting: Reflecting on the long-term implications before sharing personal photos, opinions, or information can prevent future regrets. Personal, sensitive, or potentially controversial content can affect opportunities and relationships in the future.

- Privacy Settings: Encouraging students to routinely review and update their privacy settings ensures that they have control over who can view their online activities and profiles.

The ethical use of technology transcends mere rules—it encapsulates the principles of fairness, respect, and responsibility. By ingraining these principles into our digital behaviors, we foster a more inclusive, understanding, and trustworthy online community.

Cyberbullying

The advent of the digital age has transformed the way we communicate and consume information. However, it has also introduced challenges that were previously non-existent. Among the most pervasive and detrimental is cyberbullying. Delving deeper into this issue can equip students, educators, and parents with the tools needed to tackle it effectively. The following story is from a middle school, but it is applicable at all grade levels.

It was a typical Tuesday morning when Ms. Martinez, the technology teacher at Riverview Middle School, noticed that one of her students, Emily, seemed unusually withdrawn. Normally cheerful and engaged, Emily was barely participating in class activities and kept glancing anxiously at her school-issued tablet. Concerned, Ms. Martinez decided to keep an eye on her throughout the day.

Later, during a group activity, Ms. Martinez noticed that Emily's demeanor hadn't improved. She gently approached Emily during a quiet moment and asked if everything was okay. At first, Emily hesitated, but eventually, she confided in Ms. Martinez. Emily explained that she had been receiving mean messages from a group of classmates through the school's messaging platform on her tablet. The messages were hurtful and targeted her appearance and interests.

Ms. Martinez felt a surge of empathy for Emily. She knew how devastating cyberbullying could be, especially for a sensitive middle school student. Ms. Martinez reassured Emily that she had done the right thing by speaking up and that they would handle this together. She told Emily that it was important to not respond to the bullies, to save the messages as evidence, and to block the users if possible.

Ms. Martinez promptly reported the incident to the school's administration and the guidance counselor, ensuring that the proper protocols were followed. She then arranged a meeting with Emily's parents to keep them informed and involved in the process. The school administration took immediate action to investigate the situation and address it with the students involved and their parents.

In the next technology class, Ms. Martinez decided it was crucial to address the topic of cyberbullying to the entire class. She started the lesson by discussing what cyberbullying is and how it differs from traditional bullying. She shared some statistics and real-life stories (without mentioning Emily's situation to protect her privacy) to illustrate the impact that cyberbullying can have on individuals.

Ms. Martinez then gave the students some practical advice on how to handle cyberbullying:

- **Do not respond** to the bully as it often escalates the situation.

- **Save all evidence** of bullying such as screenshots and messages.

- **Block and report** the bully on the platform where the bullying is occurring.

- **Talk to a trusted adult** about what's happening whether it's a parent, teacher, or school counselor.

She also emphasized the importance of being kind online and thinking carefully before posting or sending messages. Ms. Martinez explained that everyone has a role in creating a positive and respectful online environment and that bystanders should also speak up and support their peers if they witness cyberbullying.

The class engaged in a discussion about digital citizenship, and many students shared their thoughts and experiences. This open dialogue helped students understand the seriousness of cyberbullying and the steps they could take to prevent and address it.

By the end of the lesson, Ms. Martinez felt that the students had a better understanding of the importance of online safety and the impact of their digital actions. Emily, too, felt more supported and less isolated knowing that her teacher and classmates were there for her.

Through her proactive and compassionate approach, Ms. Martinez helped her students navigate the complexities of the digital world. She underscored the importance of kindness and empathy both online and offline.

1. Recognizing Signs and Types of Cyberbullying

- Flaming: This involves online fights, where electronic messages with angry and vulgar language are exchanged.

- Harassment: Repeated sending of malicious messages to a particular individual.

- Outing: Sharing someone's private information or secrets online without their consent.

- Exclusion: Intentionally excluding someone from an online group, like a group chat or a game.

- Impersonation: Pretending to be someone else and sending or posting material that makes that person look bad or places them in potential danger.

- Stalking: Repeated, intense harassment and denigration, including threats.

2. Strategies for Protection and Action

- Guard Personal Information: Students should be careful about what personal details they share online. They should never share their full name, location, school, or other identifiable information.

- Strong Passwords: Ensure passwords are robust and unique to prevent hacking.

- Privacy Settings: Regularly check and update the privacy settings on all social media platforms to limit who can view and post on personal profiles.

- Document and Report: If cyberbullying occurs, students should take screenshots or document the evidence and report the incidents to the relevant platform, school authorities, or even law enforcement if it's severe.

- Open Communication: Encourage students to discuss their online experiences with trusted adults. Creating an environment where they don't feel embarrassed or scared to share is vital.

3. Psychological Impact and Support Systems

- Emotional Toll: Cyberbullying can lead to anxiety, depression, low self-esteem, and in extreme cases, self-harm or suicidal thoughts.

- Physical Consequences: Victims might experience changes in sleep and eating patterns or complain of frequent headaches or stomach problems.

- Academic Impact: Decline in academic performance and increased absenteeism can be signs of being affected by cyberbullying.

- Support Structures: Schools should have counseling services equipped to handle issues of cyberbullying. Additionally, helplines, peer-support groups, and awareness programs can make a significant difference.

- Community Involvement: It's essential for the entire community, including educators, parents, and students, to be involved in anti-cyberbullying initiatives. Workshops and seminars can equip everyone with the knowledge and tools needed to combat this issue.

Confronting the menace of cyberbullying requires an integrated approach encompassing awareness, education, and compassionate support systems. By recognizing the signs and understanding the profound impact it can have, we can work towards a safer and more respectful digital community.

Chapter 26
Privacy and Security

A promising student-athlete, Jane, was set to attend a prestigious college on a full scholarship. However, a few weeks before her graduation, screenshots of racist and derogatory tweets from her past resurfaced. The aftermath was swift: her scholarship was rescinded, her acceptance revoked, and her reputation irrevocably tarnished. Jane's story serves as a poignant reminder that the Internet never forgets. What may seem like a fleeting thought or a "joke" can return to haunt individuals in unexpected ways, closing doors that once seemed wide open.

Mark was a top candidate for a high-paying tech job. His credentials were impeccable, his interview went exceptionally well, and he even had inside recommendations. However, a cursory online background check revealed controversial Facebook posts, and the offer that was almost in his grasp was given to someone else. Employers nowadays often look beyond resumes; they investigate potential employees' online presence to gauge their character and judgment. Controversial or inappropriate online content can be a deal-breaker.

Tom shared a politically charged meme on his Instagram, leading to heated arguments and a falling out with several close friends who held opposing views. While online platforms encourage sharing, not all content fosters positive interactions. Personal relationships can be strained or broken due to disagreements that start online.

In an increasingly interconnected digital age, understanding the significance of privacy and security is paramount. Every time we go online, we leave behind digital footprints. For students and educators, the stakes are even higher due to the sheer volume of digital tools used for learning and teaching. Let's delve into some key components of online privacy and security.

1. **Settings and Their Importance in Social Media Platforms and Online Tools**

   - Personal Profile Controls: Most social media platforms offer privacy settings that allow users to control who can see their posts, who can comment, and who can send them messages. Ensuring these are set to 'friends only' or 'private' can prevent unwanted attention and potential threats.

   - Data Sharing: Often, applications request access to contacts, location, and other personal data. Be selective about which apps have specific permissions to safeguard personal information.

   - Ad Preferences: Platforms often allow you to control what data is used to show ads. By managing these, you can limit targeted advertising based on your behavior and preferences.

2. **Understanding Cookies, Trackers, and Permissions**

   - Cookies: These are small files that websites place on your device to store information about your preferences or past actions. While they can make online browsing more convenient (e.g., remembering login details), they can also be used to track online activity.

   - Trackers: Websites and advertisers use these to gather information about users' browsing habits and preferences. This data can be used to build profiles that might be sold or used for targeted advertising.

   - Permissions: Many websites and apps request permission to access various features of your device (like the camera, microphone, or location). It's essential to be aware of why an app might need these permissions and only grant access when it's genuinely needed for its functionality.

3. VPNs, Two-Factor Authentication, and Other Security Measures

- VPNs (Virtual Private Networks): A VPN allows users to create a secure connection to another network over the internet. This can help shield browsing activity from prying eyes, especially on public Wi-Fi, and provide anonymity.

- Two-Factor Authentication (2FA): This is an extra layer of security used to ensure people cannot gain access to an account by only knowing the password. Typically, it involves receiving a code on a trusted device (like a phone) that needs to be entered along with the password.

- Regular Updates: Keeping operating systems, software, and apps updated ensures that you're protected from any known vulnerabilities. Developers continually release patches for newfound security threats, so regular updating is essential.

- Antivirus and Antimalware: Utilize reliable antivirus software and schedule regular scans. These tools can detect and remove malicious software that might try to steal your personal information.

By instilling a sense of digital vigilance and providing the tools and knowledge necessary to navigate the vast online realm safely, educators can empower students to make informed, responsible decisions that protect their privacy and security in the digital age.

Chapter 27
Empowerment and Activism

The digital age doesn't merely present challenges; it also offers opportunities. The same platforms that might be rife with misinformation or harassment are also avenues for change, advocacy, and collective empowerment. Today's students aren't just passive recipients of the online world; they are its architects and influencers. By embracing this potential, we can mold them into informed, passionate digital leaders. For instance, consider Greta Thunberg, who began her climate activism online using social media to amplify her voice and inspire millions globally. Her example underscores how digital platforms can be powerful tools for students to engage with critical issues and drive positive change.

In the bustling halls of Lakeside Middle School, there was a sixth-grade student named Olivia who had always been a bit shy and reserved. She was passionate about environmental issues and spent her weekends picking up litter in her neighborhood and volunteering at a local animal shelter. However, she never quite knew how to channel her passion into a broader impact.

One day, her social studies teacher, Ms. Thompson, introduced a new class project focused on digital activism. The project required students to identify a cause they cared deeply about and use digital tools to advocate for change. Ms. Thompson encouraged the students to think about the power of social media, blogs, and digital campaigns in raising awareness and mobilizing support.

Olivia's eyes lit up as Ms. Thompson spoke. She knew instantly that she wanted to focus her project on promoting environmental conservation. With Ms. Thompson's guidance, Olivia began to explore different digital platforms that could help her spread her message. She decided to create a blog to share information about environmental issues, document her community clean-up efforts, and provide tips for reducing waste and conserving resources.

Ms. Thompson also introduced Olivia to various social media platforms where she could share her blog posts and connect with like-minded individuals and organizations. Olivia learned how to create compelling graphics and videos using Canva, a user-friendly design tool, to make her posts more engaging. She also discovered how to use hashtags strategically to reach a wider audience.

As Olivia's blog gained traction, she received comments and messages from people in her community and beyond who were inspired by her efforts and wanted to get involved. She organized a community clean-up event, which was attended by dozens of volunteers who had learned about it through her digital campaign. Olivia even caught the attention of a local news station, which featured her story in a segment about young environmental activists.

Through this experience, Olivia realized the power of digital activism in amplifying her voice and making a real impact. She felt empowered and motivated to continue her advocacy work, knowing she could inspire others to join her cause.

Ms. Thompson was thrilled to see Olivia's transformation from a quiet student to a passionate digital leader. She encouraged Olivia to present her project to the school board, where she confidently shared her journey and the positive outcomes of her digital activism. The school board was so impressed that they decided to implement a school-wide initiative to promote environmental sustainability, inspired by Olivia's efforts.

Olivia's story spread throughout the school, inspiring her peers to take up their own causes and use digital tools to advocate for change. Students began to create blogs, social media campaigns, and digital petitions on various issues, from bullying prevention to mental health awareness.

Through digital empowerment and activism, Olivia and her classmates learned that they had the power to shape the world around them. They became informed and passionate digital leaders, ready to tackle the challenges of the digital age and make a positive difference in their communities.

Fostering Digital Leadership

To prevent online harassment, equip students with the understanding and tools to recognize and report online harassment, as well as to support peers who might be facing it. By fostering an environment where cyberbullying and hate are not tolerated, students can be champions of a more positive online culture.

Critical thinking should be at the core of digital navigation to battle misinformation. Encourage students to question the sources of their information, verify facts before sharing, and use platforms like MediaWise to hone their media literacy skills.

Using Online Platforms for Positive Change

Social media isn't just for selfies; it's a powerful tool for change. Students can use it to raise awareness about causes close to their hearts, from community projects to global initiatives. By showcasing real-life examples of young activists, such as Greta Thunberg's climate change movement, educators can inspire students to harness the power of digital platforms responsibly.

There are countless online communities and forums dedicated to positive change, be it environmental initiatives, social justice movements, or academic collaborations. Encourage students to join these spaces, learn from global peers, and contribute constructively.

Platforms like Change.org allow users to start petitions for causes they believe in. Students can be guided on how to effectively communicate their concerns, gather support, and present their case to relevant authorities or organizations.

When sharing content, students should be encouraged to consider the broader implications. Will this post spread positivity or negativity? Is it based on verified information? Such reflections ensure that online activism remains constructive and accurate.

The digital realm holds immense potential for activism and empowerment. By equipping students with the skills to navigate this space ethically and effectively, educators are not just preparing them for the challenges of the online world but also unlocking its myriad opportunities. The internet, after all, is what its users make of it. Let's guide our students to make it a place of informed dialogue, constructive collaboration, and impactful change.

Chapter 28
Roles of Stakeholders

In the vast and ever-evolving digital landscape, multiple stakeholders play a pivotal role in ensuring that young digital natives navigate this world with responsibility, wisdom, and care. Each stakeholder has a unique position and can contribute effectively to promote positive digital behavior.

Meet Mr. Jameson, a local business owner and parent of two middle school students. He was always passionate about technology and its potential to enhance education, but he was equally concerned about the challenges and risks it posed to young users. One evening, after attending a school board meeting where the topic of digital citizenship was discussed, Mr. Jameson felt compelled to act.

He reached out to Mrs. Hill, the school principal, expressing his interest in collaborating on initiatives to promote responsible digital behavior among students. Mrs. Hill was thrilled by his enthusiasm and suggested forming a committee comprising various stakeholders, including teachers, parents, students, and local business owners, to address the issue.

Mr. Jameson took the lead in organizing the first meeting, which included Mrs. Hill, several teachers, a few parents, and two student representatives. During this initial gathering, the group brainstormed ideas and shared their perspectives on the digital challenges students faced daily, from cyberbullying to data privacy concerns.

Recognizing the importance of a united effort, Mr. Jameson suggested partnering with local businesses to sponsor workshops and events focused on digital literacy and online safety. He reached out to fellow business owners, including the manager of a local tech company and the director of a community center, who were eager to contribute their expertise and resources.

With the support of the local tech company, the committee organized a series of workshops for students, parents, and teachers. These workshops covered topics such as creating strong passwords, recognizing phishing attempts, and maintaining a positive digital footprint. The community center offered its space for free, making it accessible to all families.

Mr. Jameson also proposed integrating digital citizenship into the school's curriculum, a suggestion that was warmly received by the teachers on the committee. They collaborated to develop lesson plans that incorporated real-life scenarios, encouraging students to think critically about their online actions and their impact on others.

To ensure that the message reached every student, the committee organized a Digital Citizenship Week featuring guest speakers, interactive activities, and a poster contest. Mr. Jameson's tech-savvy employees volunteered to lead sessions on coding and digital creativity, inspiring students to use technology positively and productively.

The student representatives played a crucial role in the initiative's success. They provided valuable insights into the challenges their peers faced and helped design a peer mentoring program where older students guided younger ones on navigating the digital world responsibly.

As the initiative gained momentum, it became clear that the collaborative effort was making a significant impact. Students became more aware of their online behavior, parents felt more confident in guiding their children's digital use, and teachers reported a noticeable improvement in students' digital literacy skills.

Mr. Jameson's dedication to the cause did not go unnoticed. The local newspaper featured an article highlighting the community's efforts to promote digital citizenship, and other schools in the district expressed interest in replicating the model.

Through the combined efforts of stakeholders like Mr. Jameson, Mrs. Hill, teachers, parents, and students, the community successfully fostered a culture of responsible digital behavior. This collaborative approach ensured that students not only embraced the opportunities offered by the digital world but also navigated it with wisdom, care, and a sense of responsibility.

Schools bear the responsibility of integrating digital citizenship into their curriculum, ensuring that students are conscious of the ethical, emotional, and societal aspects of the online world. To support this, they should provide training for faculty and staff on the latest digital tools and platforms alongside the associated challenges. Implementing robust cyber-security measures is crucial to protect student data and privacy. Embedding digital citizenship themes across various subjects is essential, whether it's understanding copyright in language arts or discussing online data in mathematics. Schools should also organize workshops and guest speaker sessions to explore the real-world implications of online behavior and encourage project-based learning where students can navigate the digital world under guided supervision.

Parents play a critical role in staying informed about the latest online platforms, apps, and games their children might be using. They should set boundaries, monitor online activities without invading privacy and engage in open conversations about the challenges and opportunities of the online world. Co-viewing or co-playing digital content with younger children and discussing it can help, as can setting up tech-free zones or times at home to ensure balanced offline and online activities. Encouraging children to share their online experiences, both positive and negative, fosters an environment of trust.

Tech companies are responsible for designing platforms and tools that prioritize user safety, especially for younger users. They should provide clear guidelines on responsible use, actively monitor and moderate content where appropriate, and be transparent about data collection, storage, and usage.

Students must understand and acknowledge the permanence of the online world and act responsibly. They should stand up against online harassment, misinformation, or any form of negative online behavior and be conscious of the time spent online, balancing it with offline activities to ensure mental and physical well-being.

It's essential to realize that digital citizenship isn't the responsibility of one group alone. It's a collaborative effort. Schools, parents, tech companies, and, most importantly, students themselves need to be proactive, informed, and engaged. Together, they can create a digital realm that's productive, safe, and respectful for everyone involved.

Section 6
Building Community

Chapter 29
Partnering with Parents in Digital Education

As the boundaries of the classroom continue to expand beyond its traditional four walls, learning intertwines more and more with our digital lives. This extension into the realm of bytes and pixels means that our mission as educators is not just to ensure students thrive academically but also to help them become adept navigators of the vast digital landscape. However, this is not a journey we can undertake alone. To create a truly impactful and lasting digital education, a collaborative approach is essential. We must bring together the influential pillars in a child's life: educators and parents.

Sarah, a parent of a middle school student named Emma, exemplifies the power of this collaborative approach. When Emma's school first introduced the iTECH model, Sarah was initially overwhelmed by the influx of digital tools and online platforms her daughter was now using. It was a significant shift from the traditional homework assignments and paper-based projects Sarah had grown up with.

Determined to support Emma, Sarah decided to immerse herself in the new digital landscape. She attended a school-organized workshop designed to familiarize parents with the iTECH model and the various technologies their children would be using. The workshop covered everything from basic digital literacy to more advanced topics like online safety and digital citizenship.

Sarah learned about the importance of monitoring online activities, setting boundaries, and having open conversations about the digital world.

One evening, Emma came to Sarah with a question about a new digital storytelling tool she was using for a school project. Instead of feeling lost, Sarah felt confident and equipped to help. She guided Emma through the steps of the iTECH model, drawing on what she had learned from the workshop. Together, they explored the app's capabilities, brainstorming creative ideas for Emma's project. This experience not only strengthened their bond but also allowed Emma to see her mother as a knowledgeable ally in her digital learning journey.

As Emma progressed through the iTECH model's phases—Inspire, Try, Expand, Create, and Huddle—Sarah remained actively involved. She encouraged Emma to share her discoveries during the Tech Talk sessions, helping her practice how to present her findings clearly and confidently. When Emma faced challenges during the Create phase, Sarah was there to provide encouragement and remind her that problem-solving and creativity often go hand-in-hand.

Sarah's involvement didn't stop at home. She joined the school's parent-teacher association and started a digital literacy committee, collaborating with other parents and educators to ensure all students had the support they needed. The committee organized regular parent workshops, created resource guides, and even set up a peer support system where more tech-savvy parents could assist those who were less familiar with the digital tools.

Through this collaborative effort, Sarah witnessed a transformation not only in Emma's digital skills but also in her confidence and enthusiasm for learning. Emma's school projects became more innovative and engaging, reflecting the dynamic interplay between traditional education and modern technology. Sarah's active participation and the partnership she fostered between parents and educators proved that when we unite our efforts, we can empower our children to navigate the digital world with skill, confidence, and creativity.

Understanding the digital world can be akin to learning a new language. For many of our students, they have grown up fluent in digital literacy, intuitively understanding its nuances and dialects. Parents, on the other hand, might feel like they are playing catch-up, grappling with an ever-evolving lexicon of apps, platforms, and digital trends. This is where educators play a pivotal role. By partnering with parents, schools can bridge the digital divide, ensuring that the lessons and values imparted in the classroom resonate and are reinforced at home.

Imagine the power and potential when home and school are perfectly synchronized in their digital education goals. This alignment can amplify positive outcomes in numerous ways:

- Consistency: Students receive consistent messages about digital responsibility, safety, and ethics both at school and at home.

- Reinforcement: Digital skills and values taught in the classroom are echoed and practiced in real-life scenarios at home, solidifying learning.

- Community: A collective approach fosters a strong sense of community, where both parents and educators share resources, strategies, and insights to support student growth in the digital domain.

This chapter will delve into the intricacies of establishing such a partnership, exploring how parents and educators can collaboratively champion the cause of comprehensive digital education. By doing so, we aren't just preparing students for exams or projects but for a future where digital prowess is intertwined with success, creativity, and innovation.

The Need for Parental Involvement

The digital world is no longer a separate entity, a distant cyberspace that we occasionally visit. It has become intertwined with our daily routines, shaping the way we communicate, work, learn, and even socialize. For today's students, the distinction between the offline and online worlds is often blurred. They grow up swiping tablets before they can write, participating in virtual classrooms, maintaining friendships across continents through chats, and navigating a plethora of online resources for homework and leisure alike. In this digital landscape, understanding how to move responsibly and effectively is as vital as any traditional subject taught in schools.

Given the ubiquity of digital tools and platforms, parents find themselves on the front lines of their children's digital experiences. Home becomes a significant arena where digital skills are put to practice, where internet ethics are tested, and where the challenges of the online realm—be it cyberbullying, misinformation, or digital addiction—might first manifest. Thus, there's an inherent need for parental involvement in digital education.

Research has consistently highlighted the profound impact of parental involvement on students' educational outcomes. When parents are actively engaged, students are more likely to:

- **Achieve Academically:** Higher grades, better attendance, and increased motivation are often associated with active parental engagement.

- **Develop Positive Attitudes:** Students with involved parents typically show a more positive attitude towards schooling and learning in general.

- **Advance to Higher Education:** Increased parental involvement often correlates with higher chances of students pursuing further education post-high school.

In the context of digital learning, parental involvement takes on an added layer of significance. A study by the National Association for Media Literacy Education emphasized that children whose parents are involved in their media and digital activities are more likely to:

- **Practice Safe Online Behaviors:** These children are less likely to share personal information or engage in risky online activities.

- **Critically Evaluate Online Content:** With guidance from parents, they are better equipped to discern between credible sources and misinformation.

- **Set Healthy Digital Boundaries:** Such children often have a more balanced digital diet and understand when to disconnect and engage in offline activities.

Given these benefits, it becomes evident that educators and parents must join forces. The insights and skills imparted in classrooms about the digital world become even more potent when echoed, reinforced, and practiced under parental guidance at home. This synergy between school and home can cultivate digitally skilled students who are responsible and critical digital citizens ready to thrive in the interconnected world of tomorrow.

Understanding the Digital Gap

The swift progression of technology over recent decades has birthed a nuanced dynamic across generations. Today's youth, who have grown up in an era rich with technology, have a different relationship with digital tools and platforms compared to many older individuals who were introduced to these technologies later in life. This variation in early-life technological experience has birthed what's commonly termed the 'digital gap.'

A middle school in Oregon recognized the hesitancy among parents when it came to digital tools. The gap between what students were learning and parents' understanding of those tools was widening.

The school organized a weekend retreat for students and their parents. The event included hands-on workshops where parents and children co-learned how to use specific educational platforms, participated in digital scavenger hunts, and even had mini competitions on who could design the most creative digital project.

Post-retreat, parents felt more comfortable assisting their kids with tech-related schoolwork. The students enjoyed the rare experience of being their parents' tech teachers. As a direct result, there was a marked increase in digital tool usage in student projects and assignments.

Parental Digital Literacy

Digital literacy goes beyond just knowing how to send an email or search the web. It embodies a thorough understanding of digital tools, online etiquette, cybersecurity protocols, and the ability to critically discern online information. Many parents, especially those from a less tech-saturated era, find this realm perplexing. The multitude of apps their children use, the intricacies of privacy settings on social media, or discerning the authenticity of online resources can be daunting terrains for them.

Early Adopters vs. Later Adopters

Rather than classifying individuals based on when they were born, it might be more accurate and sensitive to view it through the lens of adoption timing. Early adopters, typically today's youth, have seamlessly integrated technology into their daily routines and thinking patterns. They are usually at ease multitasking on digital platforms, have a penchant for visual content over text, and often thrive in connected, networked environments.

In contrast, later adopters, although they might proficiently navigate today's digital landscape, often retain habits from a time when technology wasn't as pervasive. This could manifest as a preference for print over digital content or a more sequential approach to digital tasks.

While these classifications aim to understand patterns, they are by no means rigid categories. There's a vast spectrum of digital fluency across ages, and being an early adopter doesn't necessarily equate to expertise or safe online habits.

A school district in Texas noticed that while their students were quickly adapting to the digital tools, many parents felt left behind.

Instead of the school leading the charge, they invited tech-savvy parents to lead monthly digital workshops. These sessions ranged from the basics, like setting up email accounts, to more advanced topics, such as understanding digital privacy settings.

Parents felt more involved and valued in the school community. The initiative not only bridged the knowledge gap but also fostered a sense of community among parents. With regular interactions, they started forming support groups, assisting one another in their digital learning journey.

Bridging the Gap: Strategies for Engagement

A high school in New York identified the challenge of parents struggling to understand the utility and importance of certain educational platforms and apps.

They introduced a "Tech Hour" once a month, where students would invite their parents to school. During this hour, students would present a tool or app they were using, showcasing its benefits and how it enhanced their learning. It was a platform for students to teach and parents to learn.

Not only did parents gain a deeper understanding of the tools, but students also developed a sense of ownership and pride in their learning. This simple yet effective initiative further strengthened the bond between parents, students, and technology. Here are some ways to bridge the gap:

1. **Parental Education Workshops:** Organize workshops focused on increasing digital literacy among parents. Topics can include

understanding today's popular social media, identifying online threats, and fostering healthy screen habits at home.

2. **Create Resource Centers:** Set up an online portal for parents offering resources, tutorials, and insights about the latest digital trends and their implications.

3. **Promote Collaborative Digital Exploration:** Encourage activities where children and parents explore digital tools together, sharing their insights and learning from each other.

4. **Open Lines of Communication:** Parents should be encouraged to maintain open dialogues with their children about their online experiences, discussing challenges, favorites, and more.

5. **Stay Updated:** Regularly updating devices, apps, and platforms is crucial for safety and ensures familiarity with the latest interfaces.

6. **Celebrate Digital Achievements:** Be it a parent getting the hang of a new tool or a child responsibly managing their online presence, recognizing these successes can foster further exploration and understanding.

Addressing the digital gap ensures a cohesive journey for both parents and students in the digital realm, promoting an atmosphere of mutual respect and collaboration as they navigate this evolving space.

Practical Tips for Engaging Parents

In an age where information is plentiful, but attention spans are limited, engaging parents effectively in the realm of digital education requires a thoughtful and dedicated approach. As vital stakeholders in their child's education, parents need the right resources and platforms to understand and support their child's digital journey. Here are some practical methods schools can adopt to ensure parents remain informed, involved, and invested.

Regular Digital Newsletters or Updates for Parents

1. **Content Tailored to Parents:** While schools often send out newsletters covering a range of topics, having a digital-focused newsletter can help parents quickly locate and understand the specifics of their child's digital education. These newsletters can contain insights into the latest digital tools being used, highlights of student projects, and tips for safe online practices.

2. **Interactive Elements:** Instead of a traditional text-based newsletter, consider integrating videos, clickable links, or even student-led podcast segments. This not only makes the content more engaging but also gives parents a direct taste of the digital skills their children are acquiring.

3. **Success Stories:** Share anecdotes or case studies of students who've excelled in particular digital projects, providing parents with tangible examples of the iTECH model's benefits.

Regular Parent-Teacher Conferences with a Digital Focus

1. **Digital Portfolios:** During these conferences, teachers can showcase students' digital portfolios, giving parents a firsthand look at their child's progress and accomplishments in the digital realm.

2. **Hands-on Demonstrations:** Allow parents to experience some of the digital tools and platforms their children use. This can demystify the technology and foster a deeper understanding of the curriculum.

3. **Feedback Sessions:** Dedicate a portion of these meetings to gather parental feedback on the digital curriculum, tools, or any concerns they might have.

Recommendations for User-Friendly Platforms and Apps

Provide parents with a curated list of age-appropriate apps and platforms their children are using or might find beneficial. This keeps parents in the loop and empowers them to engage in digital activities with their children.

Consider creating simple tutorials or guides for some of the more commonly used platforms. This ensures that parents who are not familiar with these tools can still support their child's digital endeavors.

Offer suggestions for digital activities that parents and children can explore together, such as building a simple website, starting a family blog, or even engaging in digital art projects.

By actively involving parents and providing them with the necessary resources and insights, schools can create a supportive environment where digital education not only thrives within classroom walls but also extends into the homes making learning a collective, community-driven endeavor.

Chapter 30
Empowering Parents as Digital Coaches

In today's interconnected world, children aren't the only ones on an educational journey. As technology continues to evolve, parents are also in a unique position to evolve alongside. Parents don't just have to be passive observers in their children's digital lives; they can become active "digital coaches," guiding, collaborating, and learning together.

Take the story of Mrs. Johnson, a dedicated mother of two elementary school children, Alex and Mia. Mrs. Johnson always felt a bit overwhelmed by the rapid pace at which technology was becoming a part of her children's education. She wanted to support their learning but felt out of touch with the tools and platforms they were using.

One evening, as Alex was struggling with a digital storytelling assignment, Mrs. Johnson decided to take a more proactive approach. She signed up for a parent workshop at their school, focused on helping parents become effective digital coaches for their children. The workshop covered the basics of the various educational technologies used, provided hands-on demonstrations, and offered strategies for parents to engage with their children in the digital space.

Equipped with new knowledge and confidence, Mrs. Johnson returned home, eager to apply what she had learned. She sat down with Alex and Mia and suggested they explore their digital tools together. They started with the storytelling app that had been causing Alex so much frustration. Instead of directing him, Mrs. Johnson guided Alex with questions and prompts, encouraging him to discover the app's features on his own.

"What do you think this button does?" she asked, sparking curiosity and critical thinking.

As they navigated the app, Mrs. Johnson shared her own learning experiences from the workshop, turning their time together into a collaborative learning session. She found that by positioning herself as a fellow learner rather than an all-knowing instructor, she created a more engaging and supportive environment for her children.

Soon, their digital coaching sessions became a regular family activity. Mrs. Johnson introduced fun challenges, like creating a family digital photo album or designing a simple game using coding platforms. She even set up a family tech night, where they would explore new educational apps and tools together. This not only enhanced Alex and Mia's digital literacy but also strengthened their family bond.

Mrs. Johnson's transformation from a passive observer to an active digital coach had a profound impact on her children's educational experience. Alex, who once dreaded digital assignments, began to approach them with enthusiasm and creativity. Inspired by her mother's willingness to learn alongside her, Mia took on more complex projects with confidence.

Moreover, Mrs. Johnson's involvement didn't go unnoticed by the school community. She began sharing her journey with other parents, encouraging them to attend the workshops and embrace their roles as digital coaches. She organized informal meetups where parents could exchange tips and experiences, fostering a supportive network.

The story of Mrs. Johnson highlights the significant role parents can play as digital coaches. By actively engaging in their children's digital education, parents can help them navigate the complexities of the online world, encourage critical thinking and creativity, and build a foundation of lifelong learning. In today's digital age, empowering parents to become digital coaches is not just beneficial, it's essential for creating a collaborative and enriching educational environment for all.

What is Digital Coaching?

At its core, digital coaching revolves around mentoring and guiding children to use technology responsibly, ethically, and productively. It's not about having all the answers or being a tech guru. Instead, it's about creating an environment where children feel supported in their digital endeavors and are encouraged to think critically and make informed choices online.

While the digital world might come more naturally to the younger generation, there's much that they can learn from their parents' life experiences, values, and perspectives. Conversely, parents can gain insights into the latest digital trends, apps, and platforms from their tech-savvy kids. This reciprocal relationship ensures that both parties grow, fostering mutual respect and understanding. Here are some ways to encourage children and parents to work together.

1. **Parent-Child Tech Days:** Allocate a day or a few hours each week where both parents and children explore a new digital tool, app, or platform together. They can take turns teaching each other about their favorite apps or digital skills.

2. **Discussion Forums:** Create spaces, either physically or digitally, where parents and students can discuss and share their online experiences, challenges, and successes.

Strategies for Active Parental Participation

Parents should embrace the mindset of continuous learning. Asking questions, showing genuine interest in the tech tools their children use, and even joining certain platforms can bridge the generational gap.

Parents and children can work together to set boundaries. Instead of imposing stringent tech rules, parents and children can collaboratively decide on screen time limits, app choices, and online behaviors, ensuring everyone has a stake in digital wellbeing.

Parents can watch media with their children. Whether it's watching a YouTube tutorial, a documentary on streaming platforms, or playing an educational game, engaging in these activities together can be both fun and educational.

Consider projects like creating a family blog, building a digital photo album, or even starting a podcast. These joint endeavors can serve as a platform for teaching, learning, and bonding.

By embracing the role of a digital coach, parents can move beyond traditional parenting paradigms and forge a new path that prepares their children for a digital future while strengthening familial bonds.

Creating a Collaborative Digital Community

As technology continues to permeate every facet of our lives, the boundaries between school and home become increasingly intertwined. The digital realm offers a unique space where educators and parents can collaboratively support students' holistic development. A collaborative digital community isn't just a benefit—it's an imperative.

The Value of School-Home Digital Initiatives

The collaboration between school and home in supporting digital learning initiatives is invaluable. By reinforcing learning at home, students receive consistent messages, aiding retention and comprehension. This holistic approach ensures students grasp not only the technical skills but also the ethical, emotional, and social aspects of digital tools. Additionally, involving parents fosters a shared responsibility, transforming digital education into a community effort rather than leaving the burden solely on educators. This cooperative model enhances the overall educational experience and supports student success.

1. **Reinforcement of Learning:** When the digital tools and skills taught in school are also embraced at home, students receive consistent messages, leading to reinforced learning and better retention.

2. **Holistic Development:** A combined effort from schools and homes ensures that students aren't just learning the technical aspects of digital tools but also the ethical, emotional, and social implications.

3. **Shared Responsibility:** Digital education is a shared venture. When parents are involved, it ensures that the responsibility doesn't lie solely with educators but is a community effort.

Open Communication Channels: Building Bridges

Establishing open communication channels between schools and homes is essential for fostering a supportive digital learning environment. Regular digital newsletters can keep parents informed about the latest classroom tools, online safety tips, and emerging digital trends. Creating feedback platforms allows parents to share their experiences and concerns, providing invaluable insights for educators. Additionally, virtual meetings via platforms like Zoom or Teams facilitate periodic discussions about digital curriculum progression, concerns, and future plans. These initiatives build bridges, ensuring a collaborative effort in supporting students' digital education.

1. **Regular Digital Newsletters:** Schools can send newsletters highlighting the latest digital tools used in classrooms, online safety tips, or new digital trends that parents should be aware of.

2. **Feedback Platforms:** Create an online forum or platform where parents can share their experiences, concerns, or suggestions regarding digital tools and curricula. This two-way communication can offer invaluable insights for educators.

3. **Virtual Meetings:** Periodic online meetings, perhaps through platforms like Zoom or Microsoft Teams, can be scheduled for parents and educators to discuss digital curriculum progression, concerns, and future plans.

Community Digital Events: Coming Together as One

Creating a strong sense of community goes beyond physical gatherings. Community digital events offer a platform for parents, students, and educators to come together, share knowledge, and strengthen their collective digital literacy. Whether it's through workshops, student showcases, or panel discussions, these events foster a collaborative environment where everyone plays an active role in enhancing the educational experience. By uniting as one, we can ensure our students are well-prepared, responsible, and empowered digital citizens.

1. **Digital Workshops for Parents:** Organizing workshops where parents can learn about the latest digital tools, online safety practices, or even basics like setting up parental controls can be incredibly beneficial.

2. **Student Showcases:** Schools can host events where students showcase their digital projects, be it a website they've designed, a digital art portfolio, or a software program they've coded. Such events can serve as a learning experience for parents and a source of pride for students.

3. **Tech Swap Days:** Organize events where parents and students can share their favorite digital tools, apps, or websites. This not only increases the community's collective digital knowledge but also strengthens bonds.

4. **Panel Discussions:** Inviting experts in the field of digital education, cybersecurity, or even tech developers for panel discussions can provide parents and educators with deeper insights into the ever-evolving digital landscape.

By fostering a collaborative digital community, we ensure that our students are receiving a well-rounded, comprehensive digital education. This collective endeavor, where parents, educators, and students all play active roles, ensures that our youth are technologically savvy, digitally responsible, and ethically grounded.

Chapter 31
Building a Community of Empowered Educators

In a quaint town nestled amidst rolling hills, there was a school not unlike many others. The classrooms were filled with chatter, laughter echoed through its corridors, and children hurried about with contagious energy. But one thing set this school apart: the teachers. These educators were on a quest, not just to teach but to inspire, innovate, and transform. They realized that while individual brilliance could light up a classroom, collective wisdom could illuminate an entire community.

Imagine this: Mrs. Smith, the social studies teacher, discovers an interactive map tool that breathes life into ancient civilizations. Down the corridor, Mr. Lee, teaching mathematics, finds a virtual lab where abstract concepts morph into tangible realities. Separately, they're game-changers, but what if Mrs. Smith shared her discovery with Mr. Lee, who then integrates historical data into his mathematical explorations? The result is a dynamic lesson where social studies and math converge, captivating young minds.

This narrative, while fictional, captures the essence of a profound truth. When educators come together as a community, they form a formidable force that transcends the boundaries of individual classrooms and subjects. In this collective spirit, the horizon of possibilities expands, bringing forth an alchemy of ideas, strategies, and innovations. Each educator becomes both a learner and a guide, contributing to and drawing from this rich tapestry of shared knowledge.

The call for such a community has never been louder. As technology relentlessly reshapes the educational landscape, it presents a cornucopia of tools designed to revolutionize the learning experience. But technology, in isolation, is like a dormant seed awaiting the right conditions to flourish. And who better to provide those conditions than a united community of passionate educators?

Our shared goal is clear: to harness the potential of technology to mold it into a powerful ally in our mission to enhance student learning. But to embark on this journey, we must remember that the path to innovation is not a solitary trek. It's a collaborative expedition where the destination becomes more attainable when we walk hand-in-hand, motivating, supporting, and uplifting each other.

Let this chapter serve as an invitation—a call to unite, collaborate, and create. For in unity, we find strength; in collaboration, innovation; and in creation, the future of education.

The Dynamic World of EdTech

The realm of educational technology is one of constant evolution. With each passing year, month, and sometimes even day, there's a wave of new tools, platforms, methodologies, and ideologies that promise to redefine the pedagogical landscape. For educators, keeping pace with these changes isn't just a luxury; it's a necessity to ensure that our students remain equipped to thrive in an ever-dynamic world.

Education and technology, when married, form a dynamic duo with the potential to bring about meaningful change. However, as with all things tech-related, the pace is swift. While this offers numerous opportunities, it can also be overwhelming. The key lies not in adopting every new trend but in discerning which trends align best with your educational objectives and the needs of your students.

The EdTech landscape is a rich tapestry of opportunities waiting to be explored. By leveraging the resources available and being proactive in our pursuit of knowledge, we can ensure that we remain at the forefront of educational innovation, perfectly poised to bring the best to our students.

The Power of Networking

The adage, "It takes a village," resonates deeply within the world of education. No educator is an island; each is a vital piece in a larger puzzle of pedagogical evolution. When educators come together, they create a symphony of diverse experiences, insights, and skills. In this context, network isn't just about professional growth. It's about propelling the entire education sector forward.

Benefits of Networking with Fellow Educators

1. **Diverse Perspectives:** Interacting with educators from varied backgrounds, specializations, and locations offers a broader perspective on teaching methodologies and strategies. Research by Dron and Anderson (2007) noted that learning within a networked collective environment leads to richer educational experiences because of the variety of views and inputs.

2. **Resource Sharing:** Networks often act as hubs for sharing resources—be it lesson plans, teaching tools, or innovative methods. This pooling of resources leads to a shared repository that can significantly enhance teaching quality.

3. **Professional Growth:** Continuous professional development is vital for any educator. Networking events, conferences, or seminars often present opportunities to learn about the latest educational trends, research, and tools.

4. **Emotional Support:** The teaching profession, while rewarding, can also be challenging. Connecting with peers provides a platform to share challenges, seek advice, or simply find a listening ear during tough times.

5. **Collaborative Opportunities:** Networking can lead to collaborative projects between schools, classes, or individual educators, fostering creativity and interdisciplinary learning.

Strategies for Effective Networking

1. **Join Professional Organizations:** Institutions such as the International Society for Technology in Education (ISTE) or the Association for Educational Communications and Technology (AECT) offer memberships, conferences, and resources dedicated to educators.

2. **Engage in Online Communities:** Platforms like EdWeb, Teachable, or The Educators PLN provide online forums and groups where educators can discuss topics, share resources, and collaborate on projects.

3. **Attend Conferences and Workshops:** Regularly participating in educational conferences, seminars, and workshops not only enhances your skill set but also provides networking opportunities with like-minded professionals.

4. **Local Educator Meetups:** Sometimes, the most valuable connections are right in your community. Look for or organize local educator

meetups or study groups.

5. **Social Media Channels:** X, with its popular education chats (like #EdChat), LinkedIn groups dedicated to education, or Pinterest boards for teachers, are excellent platforms for networking and knowledge exchange.

A Personal Invitation to the Tech Teacher Talk with Brittany Washburn Facebook Group

In our journey through the intricate web of educational technology and the iTECH model, we recognize the indispensable value of community. While the world brims with numerous platforms and forums, I'd like to extend a personal invitation to each of you reading this.

Join our vibrant community on Facebook at Tech Teacher Talk (https://www.facebook.com/groups/techteachertribe). This is more than just a group—it's a sanctuary for educators passionate about integrating technology into the classroom. It's a place where questions are welcomed, stories are shared, resources are exchanged, and the collective spirit of innovative education thrives.

Whether you're seeking advice, looking to share a success story, or simply wanting to connect with fellow tech-savvy educators, our community is your community. Together, we stay abreast of the latest in ed-tech and support and uplift one another in our shared mission: enriching the educational experience for every student in the digital age.

So, as you venture deeper into the realm of the iTECH model and explore the endless potential of educational technology, know that a community awaits you, ready to walk alongside you every step of the way. I sincerely hope to see you there, adding your unique voice to our diverse and dynamic group.

Knowledge Sharing: Workshops, Seminars, and More

In the intricate tapestry of the educational journey, every thread, every strand, counts. From the lessons meticulously planned to the dynamic of a classroom, each detail contributes to the overall experience. Among these, the collaboration of educators in platforms like workshops, seminars, and webinars shines brightly as a golden thread, weaving the fabric tighter and making it more vibrant.

The Power of Gathering

Whether it's the lively buzz in a workshop room or the collective virtual presence in an online seminar, there's unparalleled magic in gathering. It's where ideas collide, innovations are birthed, and challenges are dissected. Workshops and seminars are more than just venues for learning; they are arenas of collaboration where educators come together, united by passion and purpose.

There's an undeniable charm in the direct interactions of in-person training sessions. Teachers have the chance to shake hands with fellow educators, scribble notes while listening intently, and exchange real-time feedback. Workshops and seminars offer this—a platform to learn, unlearn, and relearn.

In a digital age, geographical boundaries blur. Online seminars or webinars provide a space where educators from different corners of the globe can converge. It offers flexibility, ensuring that distance or time constraints don't hinder the spread of knowledge.

Contribute, Collaborate, and Create

Every educator carries a reservoir of experiences, insights, and stories.

Workshops and seminars aren't just platforms to absorb; they're stages to share. Here are ways educators can contribute:

1. **Leading Sessions:** If you've pioneered a teaching method, integrated a new technology, or have insights on a particular topic, consider leading a session. Share your journey, the challenges faced, and the victories celebrated.

2. **Panel Discussions:** Joining a panel discussion can provide diverse viewpoints on a subject. It's a balanced way to both share and receive feedback, understand different perspectives, and broaden one's horizon.

3. **Interactive Workshops:** Knowledge is best retained when it's hands-on. Consider conducting a workshop where participants can engage in activities, simulations, or role-playing exercises related to your topic.

4. **Documentation and Blogging:** If public speaking isn't your forte, documenting your experiences and insights through articles or blogs can be invaluable. Share these writings in seminars, adding a fresh dimension to the discourse.

5. **Mentorship:** Often, workshops culminate in budding educators seeking guidance. Embrace the role of a mentor, guiding them through their initial steps and ensuring the legacy of quality education continues.

By actively participating in workshops and seminars, educators not only equip themselves better, but they also enrich the community. It's a symbiotic relationship where we absorb, reflect, and disseminate, ensuring that the lamp of knowledge burns brighter with every passing day.

Implementing the iTECH Model: Shared Journeys

Like most other domains, the world of education thrives on shared narratives. It is often through the lens of another's experience that we find resonance, gather inspiration, or glean insights. As we delve deeper into the integration of the iTECH model into classrooms worldwide, it's paramount to give a voice to those at the forefront of this transformative journey. Here are some anonymized reflections from educators who have embraced the iTECH model:

Testimonial 1: From Skeptic to Advocate

"When I first encountered the iTECH model, I was skeptical. My classroom had functioned perfectly well without an influx of technology. But as I delved deeper, I began to see its potential. The transformation was subtle at first—increased engagement, diverse methods of expression, and the sheer excitement on my students' faces. Over time, I've come to view technology not as a replacement but as an enhancer of my teaching. Sharing this journey with fellow educators, I realized I wasn't alone in my initial reservations, and together, we've explored and expanded on the iTECH methodology."

Testimonial 2: Breaking Barriers with iTECH

"Incorporating the iTECH model in a diverse classroom, where students hailed from varying backgrounds, was initially challenging. Yet, as days turned into weeks, I observed something beautiful: students collaborating, transcending language and cultural barriers, and using technology as a bridge. The iTECH model didn't just change the way I taught; it altered the way my students interacted, collaborated, and approached challenges."

Testimonial 3: The Continuous Evolution

"Education, in my belief, is a dynamic landscape. With the iTECH model, this belief was reaffirmed. Every day brought new insights, new tools, and new methodologies. But what remained consistent was the community's support. Through shared stories, resources, and constructive feedback, I've come to appreciate the value of collective growth and the strength in shared experiences."

These experiences emphasize the multifaceted nature of integrating technology in education. It's not just about tools or methodologies—it's about human connections, evolving pedagogy, and the shared commitment to bettering student outcomes.

Every educator's journey with the iTECH model is unique, but the underlying threads remain consistent: growth, collaboration, and continuous evolution. By sharing these journeys, we not only celebrate individual achievements but also pave the way for others, offering insights and encouragement to those poised at the brink of their own iTECH adventure.

Chapter 32
Encouraging Collaboration

Collaboration, whether among students, educators, or between schools and the community, brings immense benefits to the educational landscape. It fosters the sharing of ideas and resources, leading to enriched learning experiences and innovative teaching practices. By working together, individuals can tackle challenges more effectively, combine their strengths, and develop a deeper understanding of diverse perspectives. Collaboration also builds a sense of community and support, enhancing motivation and engagement for all involved. Ultimately, it creates a dynamic and inclusive environment where everyone can thrive and succeed.

Intra-School Collaboration

When educators within a school or district work together, share resources, and mentor each other, the entire educational ecosystem benefits, leading to enhanced teaching methods and enriched student learning experiences.

At Oakwood Elementary, the spirit of collaboration was always present. Still, it took a whole new dimension when Ms. Turner, the school principal, decided to implement a structured intra-school collaboration program. She believed that by creating more opportunities for teachers to work together, the school could leverage its staff's collective expertise and creativity to improve student outcomes.

One of the first steps Ms. Turner took was to organize bi-monthly "Collaboration Cafes." These were informal, after-school gatherings where teachers from different grades and subjects could come together, share their experiences, and discuss new ideas. To kick off the first session, Ms. Turner invited Mrs. Anderson, a fifth-grade teacher known for her innovative use of technology in the classroom, to share her experiences with the iTECH model.

Mrs. Anderson's presentation on digital stop-motion animation projects captured everyone's attention. She detailed how her students created animations to demonstrate their understanding of scientific concepts, integrating various phases of the iTECH model. Teachers from different grade levels, including kindergarten and middle school, were inspired by her methods, and started brainstorming how they could adapt similar projects for their classrooms.

Mrs. Patel, a second-grade teacher, was particularly intrigued. She approached Mrs. Anderson after the session and expressed her interest in integrating more technology into her lessons but felt unsure where to start. Mrs. Anderson offered to mentor Mrs. Patel, and they began meeting weekly to plan and co-teach a digital storytelling unit.

The collaboration didn't stop there. Recognizing the potential for cross-grade projects, Mrs. Anderson and Mrs. Patel organized a school-wide initiative where older students mentored younger ones in using digital tools. Fifth graders partnered with second graders, guiding them through the creation of simple animations and digital stories. This not only enhanced the younger students' tech skills but also fostered a sense of responsibility and leadership in the older students.

Another collaborative effort emerged when Mr. Harris, a middle school science teacher, suggested creating a shared resource library. Teachers contributed digital lesson plans, interactive activities, and project ideas they had developed. This repository became a valuable tool for teachers looking for inspiration or needing ready-to-use resources.

Ms. Turner also encouraged peer observations and feedback sessions. Teachers were invited to sit in on each other's classes, observe different teaching techniques, and provide constructive feedback. This practice created a supportive environment where teachers felt valued and empowered to try new approaches without fear of judgment.

The results of these collaborative efforts were evident in the students' engagement and performance. There was a noticeable increase in creativity, critical thinking, and enthusiasm for learning across all grades. Teachers reported feeling more connected and supported, which in turn boosted their confidence and willingness to innovate.

Ms. Turner's vision of intra-school collaboration had transformed Oakwood Elementary into a vibrant learning community where teachers and students thrived. The story of Oakwood Elementary highlights the profound impact of fostering a collaborative culture within a school, demonstrating that when educators work together, the possibilities for student success are limitless.

Strategies for Fostering Collaborative Environments

1. **Shared Vision and Goals:** Collaboration begins with a shared vision. School leadership should work with teachers and staff to establish a clear vision and goals for the school or district. Once everyone is aligned with the overall objectives, collaboration naturally follows.

2. **Open Door Policies:** Create an environment where educators can freely walk into each other's classrooms, observe, and share feedback to promote a culture of continuous learning and sharing. Such transparency can lead to organic collaboration and the cross-pollination of ideas.

3. **Collaborative Tech Platforms:** Utilizing platforms like Google Workspace for Education, Microsoft Teams, or Slack can help

teachers share resources, lesson plans, and innovative teaching techniques in real time.

4. **Team Teaching:** A method where two or more educators work together to plan, teach, and assess a single class. This fosters cooperation, and students benefit from multiple teaching styles. Here's an article (https://www.edutopia.org/practice/co-teaching-more-hands-more-learning) from Edutopia that delves deeper into the effectiveness of co-teaching.

Ideas for Regular Meetups and Resource Sharing

1. **Monthly EdCafes:** Modeled after Edcamps, schools can organize informal monthly gatherings where teachers choose the topics they wish to discuss. This grassroots movement, driven by educators for educators, ensures relevant and timely discussions.

2. **Resource Repository:** Create a centralized digital repository where teachers can upload, share, and access resources. This could be lesson plans, multimedia resources, or even classroom management tips.

3. **Mentorship Programs:** Pair experienced educators with those just starting out. Such pairings can be incredibly beneficial for both parties. While the newer teachers gain from the experience and insights of their mentors, seasoned educators get fresh perspectives and renewed energy from their mentees.

4. **Quarterly Workshops:** Organize in-house professional development sessions where teachers can present on a new tool, method, or strategy they've employed. Such workshops can act as an incubator for innovative teaching techniques.

Intra-School Collaboration:
More Than Just a Buzzword

When schools and districts recognize this and make collaboration an integral part of their ethos, the ripples of that decision positively affect every classroom and, by extension, every student.

Beyond the School Walls:
Global Collaboration

In an increasingly interconnected world, boundaries that once limited educational exchange have been dramatically expanded thanks to technological advancements. Today's educators have the unique privilege of extending collaboration beyond their immediate contexts, enriching their teaching experiences, and learning from their global peers.

Platforms for Global Collaboration

Mrs. White, a fifth-grade teacher at Meadowbrook Elementary, had always been passionate about bringing the world into her classroom. She believed that learning about different cultures and perspectives was crucial for her students. One day, while browsing through an education technology forum, Mrs. White stumbled upon an exciting idea: Mystery Skype. Intrigued by the concept, she decided to give it a try. Skype has now been discontinued, but there are still options for activities like this using platforms like Zoom, Microsoft Teams, or Google Meets.

The idea was simple yet engaging: connect with another classroom somewhere in the world via Skype and have students ask yes-or-no questions to figure out the location of the other class. Mrs. White knew this could be a fantastic way to promote global collaboration and make geography lessons come alive.

After setting up the logistics and finding a partner classroom in a different country, Mrs. White introduced the concept to her students. They were thrilled and couldn't wait to start. She divided the class into teams and assigned each group specific roles such as questioners, researchers, mappers, and recorders. This way, everyone had a part to play in the activity.

The day of the Mystery Skype session finally arrived. Mrs. White's classroom was buzzing with excitement. The students had prepared a list of questions, and the world map was prominently displayed on the smart-board, ready for action. Mrs. White connected with Mr. Ahmed's classroom in Cairo, Egypt, and the game began.

"Is your country in the Northern Hemisphere?" asked one of Mrs. White's students, nervously holding the microphone.

"Yes," came the response from the screen as Mr. Ahmed's students eagerly leaned in to listen.

The mappers quickly marked the countries in the Northern Hemisphere, while the researchers checked their notes for possible locations. The questions continued, and each team carefully strategized their next move.

"Do you have a famous river in your country?" another student asked.

"Yes, we do," answered the students from Cairo.

The excitement grew as the students zeroed in on their guesses. They discussed and debated each clue, learning to work together and think critically. Meanwhile, Mrs. White and Mr. Ahmed observed the interaction, smiling at the sight of their students learning from each other.

After several rounds of questioning, the Meadowbrook students finally pieced together the clues.

"Are you in Egypt?" one of the students asked, holding their breath.

"Yes, we are in Cairo, Egypt!" came the enthusiastic reply.

Cheers erupted in Mrs. White's classroom. The students were overjoyed and proud of their detective work. But the learning didn't stop there. They spent the remaining time sharing fun facts about their respective countries and asking more in-depth questions about each other's cultures, schools, and daily lives.

Mrs. White concluded the session with a debriefing, where the students reflected on what they had learned and how the experience had broadened their understanding of the world. They discussed the importance of asking good questions, working as a team, and appreciating different cultures.

The Mystery Skype session was a resounding success. Mrs. White saw firsthand the power of global collaboration and its positive impact on her students. They were more curious about the world, more empathetic towards people from different backgrounds, and more confident in connecting with others.

Inspired by the success of the Mystery Skype, Mrs. White decided to make it a regular part of her curriculum. She knew that by continuing to connect with classrooms around the world, she could help her students develop a global mindset and become true digital citizens.

The journey of exploration and learning continued at Meadowbrook Elementary, with each Mystery Skype session opening a new window to the world for Mrs. White's students.

Chapter 33
Overcoming Barriers to Building a Community

Building a community of empowered educators has its hurdles. Whether you're trying to foster collaboration within a school or connect with educators globally, challenges like time constraints, resistance to change, or a dearth of resources can arise. Yet, despite these obstacles, countless educators have found ways to persevere, making their collective goals a reality.

Despite the excitement surrounding the Mystery Skype session, Mrs. White encountered several barriers while setting it up. Her experience provides a roadmap for overcoming common obstacles educators might face when fostering a community of collaboration.

Firstly, Mrs. White had to navigate the challenge of time constraints. Her schedule was already packed with lessons, grading, and extracurricular activities. To find the time, she re-evaluated her weekly plan, identifying periods where traditional activities could be replaced with the more interactive Mystery Skype session. She realized that integrating this activity into her geography lessons could not only save time but also make learning more engaging. By combining subjects, she created space in her schedule without compromising the curriculum.

Another significant barrier was the initial resistance to change, both from herself and her colleagues. Mrs. White was accustomed to more traditional teaching methods and feared the chaos that could ensue from a live video session. To address these fears, she started small by incorporating minor tech tools into her lessons, gradually building her confidence and that of her students. She also attended a few professional development workshops that focused on integrating technology into the classroom. Sharing her positive experiences and small successes with her colleagues helped to mitigate their resistance. She emphasized how these tools could enhance student engagement and learning outcomes, thereby gaining their support.

The lack of resources was another hurdle. The school's tech infrastructure was not fully equipped to handle frequent video conferencing. Mrs. White approached the school administration with a proposal highlighting the educational benefits of Mystery Skype. She detailed how it could enrich the students' learning experience by providing real-world applications of their studies and promoting global awareness. Her persistence paid off, and the school allocated funds to improve the necessary tech infrastructure, including better internet connectivity and additional webcams.

Additionally, Mrs. White faced the challenge of ensuring student safety and maintaining a controlled environment during the session. She established clear guidelines and expectations for student behavior during the Mystery Skype. Before the session, she conducted mock trials to practice asking and answering questions, ensuring that students understood the format and decorum. This preparation helped create a smooth and respectful interaction during the actual session.

Furthermore, there was the technical aspect of coordinating with another classroom across the globe. Time zone differences and scheduling conflicts initially seemed daunting. Mrs. White collaborated closely with Mr. Ahmed, the teacher in Cairo, using email and planning tools to find a suitable time for both classes. They also conducted a test call to troubleshoot any technical issues beforehand, ensuring a seamless experience on the day of the session.

When the day finally arrived, Mrs. White's thorough preparation paid off. The Mystery Skype session was a success and a testament to the power of persistence and innovation. Her students were thrilled, engaged, and walked away with a deeper understanding of global cultures and geography.

By addressing these barriers head-on, Mrs. White demonstrated that with careful planning, openness to change, and a collaborative approach, even the most daunting challenges could be overcome. Her experience serves as an inspiration for educators striving to build a community of empowered learners and teachers.

Time Constraints

Between lesson planning, grading, and their myriad other duties, educators often feel they simply don't have the time to participate in extra collaborative activities or professional development sessions.

To address these issues, prioritize and start small. Dedicate a specific, manageable amount of time each week or month to community-building or professional growth. Even if it's just half an hour a week to begin with, this dedicated time can lead to significant growth and connections over the long term.

A group of teachers from various disciplines in a high school, who all faced time constraints, decided to meet for just 15 minutes every Friday after school. This "Power Quarter Hour" became a treasured time of sharing, reflection, and mutual support. Over time, these short sessions led to the development of interdisciplinary projects, sharing of resources, and enhanced camaraderie.

Resistance to Change

Some educators are wary of new methodologies or technologies, fearing they might add to their workload or disrupt their tried-and-true routines.

Those comfortable with technology can offer hands-on training sessions, provide mentorship, and emphasize the benefits for both teachers and students. Lead by example and celebrate the small victories.

At a mid-sized elementary school, the introduction of a new digital learning platform was met with skepticism. However, after a few teachers volunteered to pilot the program and showcased their successes in staff meetings, the atmosphere began to shift. These early adopters became in-house mentors, guiding their colleagues through the platform and turning skeptics into proponents.

Lack of Resources

Limited budgets or resources can sometimes hamper community-building or technology integration efforts.

To gain resources, think outside the box. Use free online resources, tap into local expertise, and look for grants or partnerships to fund initiatives. Often, communities possess hidden talents or resources that can be harnessed if you know where to look.

When a rural school district faced budget constraints that threatened its EdTech initiatives, they turned to the community. Local businesses sponsored tech tools in exchange for students showcasing their projects or skills at company events. Not only did this solve the funding issue, but it also strengthened bonds between the school and the broader community.

Every challenge presents an opportunity in disguise. Though dotted with obstacles, the path to building a robust community of educators is paved with potential triumphs. By focusing on solutions, learning from success stories, and rallying around shared goals, barriers can be transformed into steppingstones toward a brighter, more collaborative future.

Section 7
Educational Policy and Technology

Chapter 34
Educational Policy and the Digital Classroom: Implications for Policymakers

Gone are the days when chalkboards and textbooks defined the learning environment. Today, digital technology is ubiquitous in classrooms, from interactive whiteboards to tablets and from online resources to sophisticated learning management systems. This digital integration promises personalized learning experiences, greater access to information, and innovative teaching methodologies. However, with these advancements come questions about equity, accessibility, and our education systems' readiness to fully harness the potential of these technologies.

The Critical Need for Informed Policymaking

As educational technology continues to advance, policymakers are tasked with a critical responsibility: to create frameworks that not only accommodate these changes but also actively foster an environment where technology enhances education effectively and equitably. This requires policies that go beyond mere infrastructure and hardware provision. We need strategies that address teacher training, curriculum development, student data privacy, and the digital divide, ensuring that every student benefits from these technological advancements.

The Intersection of Technology and Policy

The intersection of educational technology and policy is where practicality meets vision. Policies shape how technology is implemented, who has access to it, and how its impact is measured and enhanced. Conversely, the fast-paced evolution of technology constantly redefines what is possible in education, challenging policymakers to stay adaptive and proactive. This symbiosis between technology and policy is the fulcrum on which the future of education balances.

Policy needs to anticipate and guide the integration of technology in education. We will examine the challenges policymakers face, the opportunities that lie ahead, and the strategies that can bridge the gap between the potential of technology and the realities of our education systems.

As we embark on this journey, it's important to remember that at the heart of every policy, every decision, and every technological tool, the ultimate goal is to enrich and empower our students, the future citizens of an increasingly digital world.

Chapter 35
Current State of Educational Technology

The landscape of educational technology policies is as diverse as it is dynamic, spanning across local, state, national, and international spectrums. These policies form the backbone of how educational technology is integrated into classrooms, impacting everything from the tools used to the methods of instruction.

Local and State Level Policies

At the local and state levels, policies often focus on the implementation and funding of technology in schools. These policies can vary significantly based on the region's economic resources and educational priorities. For instance, a study by the Consortium for School Networking (CoSN) revealed that while some districts prioritize investments in high-speed internet and one-to-one device programs, others focus more on teacher training for digital learning.[5] These differences profoundly affect the nature and efficacy of technology integration in classrooms.

The impact of local and state policies on schools' technology integration

---

5 Consortium for School Networking (CoSN), *2021 EdTech Trends Report* (Washington, DC: CoSN, 2021).

can be profound and multifaceted. Here are some examples illustrating how these policies shape educational environments.

1. **High-Speed Internet Access:** In districts where policies prioritize high-speed internet access, students benefit from seamless connectivity, enabling them to access a plethora of online resources and learning tools. For instance, in rural areas where broadband access has been historically limited, initiatives like the FCC's E-rate program provide discounts to help schools and libraries obtain affordable telecommunications and internet access. This ensures students in these regions have the same opportunities as their urban counterparts.

2. **One-to-One Device Programs:** Policies that fund one-to-one device programs equip each student with a personal device, such as a laptop or tablet. For example, Maine's Learning Technology Initiative has provided laptops to middle school students since 2002, significantly enhancing digital literacy and learning outcomes. These programs ensure that all students, regardless of socioeconomic status, have access to the digital tools necessary for modern education.

3. **Teacher Training for Digital Learning:** Some districts emphasize professional development to ensure teachers are well-equipped to integrate technology into their classrooms effectively. For example, the state of Texas has implemented the Texas Technology Applications Standards, requiring teacher preparation programs to include technology integration strategies. This focus on teacher training helps educators to better utilize digital tools, creating more interactive and engaging learning environments.

4. **Digital Equity and Inclusion:** Policies that address digital equity ensure all students have access to technology, regardless of their background. For instance, California's Broadband Infrastructure Improvement

Grant program aims to close the digital divide by providing high-speed internet to underserved schools. This ensures that every student has the opportunity to benefit from digital learning resources.

5. **Blended Learning Models:** In some regions, policies support the development of blended learning models, which combine online digital media with traditional classroom methods. For example, New York's Smart Schools Bond Act allocated funds to improve educational technology and infrastructure, enabling schools to implement blended learning environments. This approach allows for personalized learning experiences and greater flexibility in how students engage with content.

6. **STEM and Coding Initiatives:** Certain policies focus on promoting STEM (Science, Technology, Engineering, and Mathematics) education and coding skills. For example, the state of Arkansas passed legislation requiring all public high schools to offer computer science courses, reflecting a commitment to preparing students for the future job market. Such policies ensure students develop critical skills needed in a technology-driven world.

These examples highlight how local and state policies can significantly influence technology integration in schools, impacting everything from internet access and device availability to teacher training and curriculum development. By addressing these various facets, policies can help create more equitable, effective, and innovative educational environments.

National Level

On a national scale, policies tend to address broader issues such as digital equity, curriculum standards for technology education, and student data privacy. In the United States, initiatives like the Every Student Succeeds Act (ESSA) have provided guidelines and funding for educational technology, emphasizing the need for equitable access. The National Education Technology Plan, updated periodically by the US Department of Education, serves as a comprehensive guide for educators and policymakers, highlighting the need for robust infrastructure, digital literacy, and innovative teaching practices.[6]

International Perspective

Globally, UNESCO's Qingdao Declaration outlines a commitment to harness the power of information and communication technology (ICT) to achieve quality, inclusive, and equitable education for all. Similarly, the European Commission has developed policies like the Digital Education Action Plan, which aims to foster digital literacy and learning through technology across European Union member states.[7]

Shaping Digital Classroom Environments

These varying levels of policies directly shape digital classroom environments. They influence not only the type of technology available in schools but also how it is utilized in the educational process. For instance, a policy emphasizing digital literacy will likely lead to classrooms where technology is used as a tool for creating and problem-solving rather than solely for information consumption.

---

6 U.S. Department of Education, *A Call to Action for Closing the Digital Access, Design, and Use Divides: 2024 National Educational Technology Plan* (Washington, DC: Office of Educational Technology, 2024), https://tech.ed.gov/netp/.

7 UNESCO. *Qingdao Declaration: Seize Digital Opportunities, Lead Education Transformation.* Paris: UNESCO, 2015. https://unesdoc.unesco.org/ark:/48223/pf0000233352.

Furthermore, policies regarding student data privacy and cybersecurity, such as the General Data Protection Regulation (GDPR) in the EU, are shaping how technology is managed in schools.[8] They ensure that while schools embrace digital learning, they also safeguard students' personal information.

The current state of educational technology policies reflects a diverse and evolving landscape. While there is a general global trend towards embracing and integrating technology in education, the approaches and focuses differ significantly. These policies, at various levels, not only dictate the availability and type of technology in schools but also influence the pedagogical approaches and the overall learning environment. As technology continues to advance, it's crucial for these policies to be regularly revisited and adapted to ensure they meet the changing needs of educators and students alike.

---

8   European Commission, Digital Education Action Plan 2021–2027: *Resetting Education and Training for the Digital Age* (Brussels: European Commission, 2020), https://education.ec.europa.eu/focus-topics/digital-education/action-plan.

Chapter 36
Challenges and Opportunities for Policymakers

As policymakers grapple with the integration of digital technology in educational settings, they encounter a spectrum of challenges, each presenting unique opportunities. The key lies in recognizing these challenges not as roadblocks but as catalysts for progressive change.

Challenges Faced by Policymakers

Policymakers in the realm of educational technology face a myriad of challenges that can hinder the effective implementation and integration of digital tools in schools. The rapid pace of technological advancements often leaves policies outdated, creating a gap between current technology and educational needs. Addressing the digital divide and ensuring equitable access to technology across different socio-economic and geographical regions remains a pressing concern. Additionally, the necessity for comprehensive training and professional development for educators, coupled with funding constraints, further complicates the landscape. Finally, the increasing focus on data privacy and cybersecurity adds another layer of complexity that policymakers must navigate to protect students while fostering digital learning environments.

1. **Keeping Pace with Technological Advances:** The rapid evolution of technology presents a significant challenge. Policies often lag behind the latest technological developments which leads to a mismatch between available resources and educational needs.

2. **Digital Divide and Equity:** One of the most pressing issues is the digital divide. Access to technology varies greatly across different socio-economic and geographical regions which leads to disparities in educational opportunities.

3. **Training and Professional Development:** The successful integration of technology requires educators to be proficient in using these tools. However, there's often a gap in the required training and professional development for teachers. This hampers effective technology integration.

4. **Funding and Budget Constraints:** Allocating adequate funds for technological resources, training, and maintenance is a perennial challenge for policymakers. Budget constraints can limit the scope and reach of digital education initiatives.

5. **Data Privacy and Cybersecurity:** As schools increasingly incorporate technology, concerns about student data privacy and cybersecurity grow. Policymakers must navigate these complex issues to protect students while promoting digital learning.

Opportunities for Policymakers

While the challenges for policymakers in integrating digital technology into education are manifold, each challenge also presents a unique opportunity to shape a more inclusive, effective, and dynamic educational landscape.

1. **Promoting Innovation through Policy:** By creating policies that encourage and fund innovation in educational technology, policymakers can foster a culture of creative problem-solving and technological advancement.

2. **Bridging the Digital Divide:** Policies focused on equitable access to technology can help bridge the digital divide. This includes investing in infrastructure, providing devices, and ensuring high-speed internet access, especially in underserved communities.

3. **Emphasizing Teacher Training:** Investing in comprehensive teacher training programs can maximize the benefits of technology in education. Policies can support professional development initiatives that empower teachers to integrate technology effectively.

4. **Flexible and Forward-Thinking Policies:** Adopting a flexible approach to policymaking allows for quicker adaptation to technological changes. This includes regularly revisiting and updating policies as technology evolves.

5. **Prioritizing Data Security and Ethics:** Establishing clear guidelines and standards for data privacy and security in educational technology can build trust and ensure a safe learning environment for students.

6. **Collaboration with Tech Industry and Educators:** Policymakers have the opportunity to collaborate with technology experts and educators. Such partnerships can lead to developing relevant, effective, and user-friendly educational technologies.

By addressing these challenges head-on, policymakers can significantly influence the trajectory of educational technology, ensuring it serves as a powerful tool for learning and development.

Chapter 37
Impact of Policy on Classroom Practices

The intricate web of educational policies wields a profound influence on classroom practices, teacher training, and student learning experiences. These policies, whether directly targeting classroom dynamics or indirectly influencing educational frameworks, set the tone for how education is delivered and experienced.

Direct Impact on Classroom Practices

Policies directly targeting the use of technology in classrooms can shape the daily experiences of both teachers and students. For example, a policy mandating the use of specific learning management systems (LMS) can dictate the structure of lesson delivery, student assessment, and even classroom interaction. A case in point is the implementation of the Common Core State Standards in the United States, which led to an increased adoption of digital tools for assessment and personalized learning, directly impacting teaching methods and student engagement.

Teacher Training and Professional Development

Educational policies often include provisions for teacher training, which is crucial for effective technology integration. For instance, the European Commission's Digital Education Action Plan emphasizes enhancing digital competencies for educators. This policy led to the development of various training programs across Europe, equipping teachers with skills necessary for the digital age, thereby transforming traditional teaching methodologies.

Indirect Influence on Student Learning Experiences

Policies can also indirectly influence student learning. For example, policies emphasizing STEM education have led schools to integrate more technology-based learning in science and mathematics. This shift not only changes the subject focus but also encourages the use of digital tools, promoting a more interactive and engaging learning environment.

Case Studies

1. Singapore's Technology-Driven Curriculum: Singapore's Ministry of Education implemented a policy to integrate technology across all levels of education. This led to the development of the FutureSchools project, where selected schools received funding to experiment with new teaching methods and technology. The outcome was a significant improvement in student engagement and academic performance, as

reported in a study by the National Institute of Education, Singapore.

2. Finland's Flexible Education Policy: Finland's approach to education policy, known for its flexibility and teacher autonomy, allows educators to integrate technology as they see fit. This policy has cultivated a culture of innovation in classrooms, with teachers freely experimenting with digital tools to enhance learning, as highlighted in several OECD reports.

In essence, educational policies, whether through direct mandates or indirect incentives, profoundly shape the landscape of classroom practices. They can dictate the tools and methods teachers use, the way students interact with content, and the overall learning atmosphere. As such, policy-makers carry the responsibility to craft policies that not only keep pace with technological advancements but also prioritize the needs and potential of both educators and students in the digital age.

Aligning Policy with Pedagogical Goals

It is crucial that policymaking does not occur in a vacuum. Instead, it should be intricately woven with the broader pedagogical goals and educational standards that guide our educational systems. Such alignment ensures that technology is not just an add-on but a significant enhancer of the learning process.

Educational technology policies must resonate with the overarching objectives of education: to foster critical thinking, creativity, collaboration, and communication among students. This alignment is pivotal in ensuring that technology integration in the classroom is meaningful, purposeful, and directed toward the holistic development of learners.

Strategies for Policymakers

The alignment of educational technology policies with pedagogical goals is not just a strategic imperative but a moral one. It ensures that technology integration in education is thoughtful, inclusive, and directed towards enriching the learning experience for all students.

1. **Engage with Educational Stakeholders:** Policymakers should collaborate with teachers, administrators, curriculum developers, and even students to understand the ground realities of classroom learning. This will help in crafting policies that are practical, relevant, and supportive of pedagogical objectives.

2. **Focus on Teacher Empowerment:** Policies should include provisions for comprehensive teacher training and professional development. By equipping teachers with the necessary skills and knowledge to integrate technology effectively, policies can directly influence the quality of teaching and learning.

3. **Curriculum Integration:** Technology policies should advocate for the integration of digital tools that complement and enhance the existing curriculum. This might involve revising curriculum standards to include digital literacy ensuring that technology use aligns with educational goals.

4. **Regular Policy Reviews and Updates:** Educational technology is a field marked by rapid changes. Policies need to be revisited and revised regularly to remain relevant and effective. This process should be guided by feedback from educational practitioners and the latest research in pedagogy and technology.

5. **Promote Research-Based Practices:** Policies should be grounded in

educational research and best practices. Encouraging pilot programs and case studies can provide valuable insights into how technology can best serve pedagogical goals.

6. **Ensure Equitable Access:** Policies must ensure that all students, regardless of their background, have equal access to technological resources. This aligns with the broader educational goal of providing equitable learning opportunities to every student.

For policymakers, this alignment is a guiding principle that ensures technology serves as a bridge, not a barrier, in achieving educational objectives.

Chapter 38
Inclusivity and Accessibility in Policymaking

In an era where education is increasingly intertwined with technology, it is imperative that educational policies champion the principles of inclusivity and accessibility. Every student, regardless of their socio-economic background, geographic location, or physical and cognitive abilities, deserves equitable access to technology and the rich educational opportunities it offers.

In a small, rural community, there was a school named Pine Hill Elementary. The students and teachers at Pine Hill were passionate about learning and dedicated to making the most of their educational experiences. However, despite their enthusiasm, the school faced significant challenges due to a lack of access to modern technology.

Mrs. Johnson, a fifth-grade teacher at Pine Hill, had heard about the benefits of incorporating digital tools into the classroom. She knew technology could open doors to new learning opportunities, enhance student engagement, and better prepare her students for the future. Unfortunately, the school's budget constraints and outdated infrastructure made it difficult to obtain necessary resources.

One day, Mrs. Johnson learned about a free online coding program that could teach her students valuable skills in programming and critical thinking. Excited by the possibilities, she planned a lesson around this resource. However, when she brought her class to the computer lab, she was met with a harsh reality: most of the computers were outdated, slow, and unable to support the coding software. The few functional computers were constantly in use, shared among multiple classes, and often required repair.

The students, eager to learn, tried their best to follow along with Mrs. Johnson's instructions. They crowded around the few working computers, taking turns and trying to help one another. Despite their best efforts, the slow loading times and frequent crashes made it nearly impossible to complete lessons. Frustration grew as the students realized they were missing out on the chance to explore coding, a skill that could have opened doors to countless future opportunities.

One of Mrs. Johnson's brightest students, Emily, had always shown a keen interest in technology. She had dreams of becoming a software engineer, but without access to the necessary tools and resources, she felt her dreams slipping further away. Emily confided in Mrs. Johnson, expressing her concerns and disappointment. Mrs. Johnson, feeling equally disheartened, assured Emily that she would continue to seek out ways to bring technology into their classroom.

Determined to make a difference, Mrs. Johnson began writing grant proposals and reaching out to local businesses for support. She even organized a fundraiser to gather donations for new equipment. While her efforts were commendable, the process was slow, and the funds raised were insufficient to provide the comprehensive technological upgrades the school desperately needed.

As the school year progressed, Pine Hill's lack of access to modern technology became more evident. Students struggled to complete research projects, missed out on interactive science simulations, and were unable to participate in virtual field trips that other schools enjoyed. The digital divide was glaring, and it was clear that Pine Hill's students were at a significant disadvantage compared to their peers in better-equipped schools.

The experience at Pine Hill Elementary highlighted the critical need for educational policies that prioritize inclusivity and accessibility. Without equitable access to technology, students like Emily were missing out on essential learning opportunities and the chance to develop skills that would be vital in their future careers. The story of Pine Hill serves as a poignant reminder that bridging the digital divide is not just about providing devices and internet access; it's about ensuring that every student has the opportunity to thrive in a technology-rich educational environment.

Ensuring Equitable Access

The gap between those with and without access to modern information and communication technology, known as the digital divide, poses a significant challenge in the realm of education. To bridge this divide, policies must address the following issues:

1. **Address Infrastructure Disparities:** Ensure that all schools, especially those in rural or underserved areas, have access to high-speed internet and modern digital infrastructure. This might involve allocating funds specifically for technological upgrades in these areas.

2. **Provide Devices:** Implement programs that provide laptops, tablets, or other necessary devices to students who cannot afford them. This ensures that no student is left behind due to a lack of resources.

3. **Support Home Access:** Recognize that access to technology should not end at the school gate. Policies should support initiatives that provide students with the necessary technology and internet access at home, particularly in low-income households.

Incorporating Accessibility for Students with Disabilities

For students with disabilities, digital technology can be a powerful tool to enhance learning, provided it is accessible. To make policies effective for all students, use the following strategies.

1. **Mandate Accessibility Standards:** Ensure that all educational technology complies with accessibility standards, making them usable for students with various disabilities.

2. **Specialized Tools and Resources:** Invest in and provide specialized technological tools and resources, such as screen readers, speech-to-text software, or Braille displays, to meet the specific needs of students with disabilities.

3. **Teacher Training:** Include provisions for training teachers in using assistive technologies and implementing inclusive teaching practices that effectively leverage technology.

Examples of Effective Policies

The following examples demonstrate how effective policies can make a significant difference in providing equitable educational opportunities for students with disabilities. By prioritizing accessibility and inclusivity, these regions ensure that all students have the tools and support they need to succeed in a digital learning environment.

California, USA

Known for its comprehensive policies supporting students with disabilities,

California has implemented several initiatives to promote accessibility in education. The state has established the California Assistive Technology System (CATS) to provide resources and support for integrating assistive technology in schools.[9] Additionally, California mandates that all educational materials and digital content meet accessibility standards, ensuring students with disabilities have equal access to learning resources.

England, UK

The UK has robust policies to support students with disabilities, including the Special Educational Needs and Disability (SEND) Code of Practice.[10] This framework ensures that schools are equipped with the necessary technology and support systems to provide inclusive education. England has also invested in training programs for teachers to effectively use assistive technology and adapt teaching methods to meet the diverse needs of students.

New South Wales, Australia

The NSW Government has made significant strides in supporting students with disabilities through the Digital Education Revolution initiative.[10] This program aims to provide every student access to digital learning tools and resources. Additionally, the state has implemented policies to ensure that all educational websites and online platforms comply with accessibility standards, making it easier for students with disabilities to engage with digital content.

Finland, Europe

Finland is often highlighted for its inclusive education policies. The country

9   UNESCO, *Leveraging Information and Communication Technologies to Achieve the Post-2015 Education Goal* (Paris: UNESCO, 2020), https://unesdoc.unesco.org/ark:/48223/pf0000373656.

10   Francesca Gottschalk and Crystal Weise, *Digital Equity and Inclusion in Education: An Overview of Practice and Policy in OECD Countries,* OECD Education Working Paper No. 299 (Paris: OECD Publishing, 2023), https://one.oecd.org/document/EDU/WKP(2023)14/en/pdf.

has integrated assistive technology into its national education framework, ensuring that students with disabilities have access to the same learning opportunities as their peers.[10] Finnish schools are equipped with various assistive devices and software, and there is a strong emphasis on personalized learning plans to meet the individual needs of each student.

Cultural and Linguistic Inclusivity

Educational technology should also respect and represent the cultural and linguistic diversity of the student population. Here are some strategies to create policies that nurture cultural and linguistic diversity.

1. **Promote Multilingual Resources:** Encourage the development and use of educational resources in multiple languages, ensuring that language is not a barrier to accessing technology-driven education.

2. **Culturally Responsive Content:** Advocate for and support the creation of digital content that is culturally inclusive and sensitive, reflecting the diverse backgrounds of students.

Inclusive and accessible educational technology policies are not just about ensuring every student has a device or an internet connection. They are about making sure that every aspect of technology integration in education, from infrastructure to content, is thoughtfully designed to meet the diverse needs of all learners. Such policies affirm the commitment to an equitable, just, and inclusive educational landscape where technology acts as a bridge, not a barrier, to learning.

Chapter 39
Funding and Resource Allocation

The seamless integration of educational technology hinges significantly on the strategic funding and allocation of resources. Policies at various levels play a critical role in ensuring that financial and infrastructural support aligns with the educational objectives of integrating technology in classrooms. This section will explore the nuances of funding and resource allocation, offering insights into effective budgeting strategies and financial models that can bolster digital education.

At Green Valley High School, the successful integration of educational technology can be attributed to strategic funding and careful allocation of resources. These same strategies can be applied to any schools. The school district recognized early on that to prepare students for the digital age, significant investment in technology infrastructure was necessary.

Three years ago, the district applied for a state grant specifically aimed at enhancing digital learning environments. This grant provided a substantial initial investment, enabling Green Valley High School to purchase laptops for every student and install high-speed internet across the campus. To ensure sustainable funding, the district also reallocated portions of its existing budget by identifying and reducing expenditures on outdated educational materials and reallocating those funds toward technology.

In addition to state funding, the school sought partnerships with local businesses and technology companies. These partnerships not only provided additional financial support but also brought in expertise and professional development opportunities for teachers. For example, a local tech firm sponsored coding workshops and provided mentorship programs for students interested in STEM fields.

To maximize the impact of their investments, Green Valley High School implemented a comprehensive plan to integrate technology into the curriculum. This included purchasing educational software licenses, setting up a digital learning platform, and offering regular training sessions for teachers. The school also established a technology committee of teachers, administrators, and IT specialists to oversee the ongoing maintenance and upgrading of technological resources.

Through strategic funding and resource allocation, Green Valley High School has created a technology-rich learning environment that supports innovative teaching practices and enhances student engagement. This example illustrates the critical role of thoughtful budgeting and financial planning in the seamless integration of educational technology, ensuring that investments align with the broader educational objectives of the school.

Policy's Role in Funding Educational Technology

Funding educational technology is a critical aspect that can significantly influence the quality and reach of digital learning initiatives. Effective policies play a crucial role in directing resources and establishing financial frameworks to support these technological advancements in education. This section explores how policy can set priorities for funding, create grants and special funding programs, and encourage public-private partnerships. By strategically leveraging these mechanisms, policymakers can ensure that schools and districts have the necessary financial support to integrate and sustain educational technology effectively.

1. **Setting Priorities:** Policies dictate where and how funds are allocated. By prioritizing educational technology, policymakers can channel funds toward necessary infrastructure, devices, and training programs.

2. **Grants and Funding Programs:** Implementing policies that establish grants or special funding programs for technology in education can provide essential financial support to schools and districts, especially those with limited budgets.

3. **Public-Private Partnerships (PPPs):** Encouraging PPPs can be a strategic way to fund educational technology initiatives. These partnerships can leverage private sector expertise and resources, reducing the financial burden on public institutions.

Effective Budgeting Strategies

Effective budgeting is a cornerstone of successful educational technology integration. As schools and districts strive to enhance their digital capabilities, it is essential to allocate resources wisely to ensure sustainability and maximize impact. This section delves into strategic budgeting practices that can help educational institutions make informed and efficient financial decisions. By conducting needs assessments, performing cost-benefit analyses, and planning for the long term, schools can optimize their investments in technology to better support teaching and learning objectives.

1. **Needs Assessment:** Conduct thorough needs assessments to determine the specific technological requirements of each school or district. This ensures that spending is targeted and efficient.

2. **Cost-Benefit Analysis:** Before allocating funds, perform a cost-benefit analysis to evaluate the potential impact and sustainability of

technology investments. This approach ensures that investments yield tangible educational benefits.

3. **Long-term Planning:** Incorporate technology spending into long-term budget planning. This includes not only the initial procurement of technology but also ongoing costs like maintenance, upgrades, and training.

Financial Models Supporting Digital Education

The role of policy in funding and resource allocation for educational technology cannot be overstated. Effective policies coupled with strategic financial planning and innovative funding models can significantly enhance the scope and quality of technology integration in education.

1. **Earmarked Funds:** Setting aside a specific portion of the education budget for technology ensures consistent funding. This can be particularly effective at the state or national level.

2. **Tiered Funding Models:** Implementing a tiered funding model can address the varying needs of schools. Schools in higher-need areas might receive additional funding to bridge the digital divide.

3. **Innovative Financing:** Exploring innovative financing methods like social impact bonds or education savings accounts can provide alternative sources of funding for educational technology.

4. **Crowdfunding and Community Involvement:** Encouraging schools to engage in crowdfunding campaigns or community fundraising activities can supplement traditional funding sources.

Such financial foresight and commitment are essential in ensuring that all students have access to the tools and resources necessary to thrive in a digital world.

Chapter 40
Data Privacy and Security

In an era where educational technology is ubiquitous, the protection of student data emerges as a paramount concern. The intersection of education and digital platforms creates vast reservoirs of sensitive information, making data privacy and security-critical components of any educational technology policy.

The Importance of Data Privacy and Security in EdTech Policies

With the increasing digitalization of education, students' personal information, learning records, and even behavioral data are often stored and processed through various digital platforms. This data, if mishandled, can lead to significant privacy breaches and security risks. Policies focusing on data privacy and security ensure the safe use of technology, which protects students, and maintains trust in educational systems.

Current Challenges in Data Privacy and Security

As educational institutions increasingly integrate digital tools and technologies, they face significant challenges in safeguarding the privacy and security of student data. The potential exposure of sensitive information through cyberattacks is a growing concern, making schools vulnerable targets. Moreover, navigating complex data protection regulations like GDPR and FERPA can be overwhelming, particularly for institutions with limited resources. Adding to this challenge is a general lack of awareness among educators and students about best practices for data protection, further heightening the risk of breaches or data misuse.

1. **Vulnerability to Data Breaches:** Schools and educational institutions are increasingly becoming targets for cyberattacks, leading to the potential exposure of sensitive data.

2. **Compliance with Regulations:** Adhering to data protection regulations, such as the General Data Protection Regulation (GDPR) in the EU or the Family Educational Rights and Privacy Act (FERPA) in the US, can be complex and challenging, especially for institutions with limited resources.

3. **Lack of Awareness:** Often, educators and students are unaware of the best practices for data protection, increasing the risk of accidental breaches or misuse of data.

Navigating Data Privacy and Security Challenges in an Educational Institution

In the bustling city of Harborview, a public high school named Ridgewood High was a beacon of academic excellence. With a progressive administration and an enthusiastic teaching staff, the school was an early adopter of educational technology. They integrated digital tools into their classrooms, offering students the advantages of modern learning resources. However, along with these advancements came significant challenges related to data privacy and security.

The first major challenge arose one fall afternoon when the school's IT administrator, Mr. Harrison, detected unusual activity on the network. A thorough investigation revealed that the school's database had been compromised by a cyberattack, potentially exposing sensitive student and staff data. This breach sent shockwaves through the school community. Personal information, including grades, contact details, and even health records, were at risk. The administration quickly notified affected individuals and began working with cybersecurity experts to mitigate the damage.

In the wake of the breach, Principal Martinez realized the importance of adhering to stringent data protection regulations. She convened a task force, including legal experts and tech consultants, to ensure that Ridgewood High complied with relevant laws such as the Family Educational Rights and Privacy Act (FERPA) in the US. The task force discovered gaps in their current practices, which necessitated immediate changes. They updated their data storage policies, encrypted all sensitive information, and implemented regular audits to ensure ongoing compliance. However, this process was time-consuming and resource-intensive, straining the school's limited budget and staff.

Despite these efforts, one of the most significant hurdles was the general lack of awareness among educators and students about best practices for data protection. To address this, Mr. Harrison organized a series of workshops aimed at educating the school community. During these sessions, teachers learned about creating strong passwords, recognizing phishing emails, and safely storing digital records. Students were taught the importance of data privacy, how to safeguard their personal information online, and the ethical use of technology.

In one memorable workshop, Ms. Jenkins, a math teacher, shared an eye-opening experience. She recounted receiving a seemingly innocent email asking her to confirm her login details for the school's grading system. Trusting the email, she complied, only to realize later that it was a phishing attempt. This story resonated with many colleagues and students and high-lighted the real risks of cyber threats and the importance of vigilance.

Through these collective efforts, Ridgewood High School gradually strengthened its defenses against data breaches, improved its compliance with legal regulations, and raised awareness about data privacy. The journey was fraught with challenges, but it underscored the critical importance of data security in today's digital age, and it ultimately made the school a safer place for everyone.

This story of Ridgewood High exemplifies the pressing need for schools to prioritize data privacy and security. By acknowledging vulnerabilities, striving for regulatory compliance, and fostering a culture of awareness, educational institutions can better protect their communities from the ever-evolving landscape of digital threats.

Guidelines and Considerations for Policymakers

Policymakers play a crucial role in framing the laws and regulations that guide the safe, ethical use of educational technology which safeguards the interests and well-being of students.

1. **Establish Clear Data Protection Policies:** Create and enforce comprehensive data privacy policies that dictate how student data is collected, used, stored, and shared. These policies should be transparent and accessible to educators, students, and parents.

2. **Regular Training and Awareness Programs:** Implement ongoing training programs for educators, administrators, and students on data privacy and cybersecurity best practices.

3. **Ensure Compliance with Legal Standards:** Policies should be aligned with national and international data protection laws. Regular audits and updates are crucial to ensure compliance with these evolving regulations.

4. **Invest in Secure Infrastructure:** Allocate funds for secure and up-to-date technological infrastructure that prioritizes data security, including encrypted systems and secure cloud storage solutions.

5. **Promote a Culture of Privacy:** Encourage an educational culture that values and protects privacy. This includes both technical measures and fostering responsible attitudes and behaviors regarding data among all stakeholders.

6. **Involve All Stakeholders:** Develop these policies in consultation with educators, IT professionals, legal experts, and community representatives to ensure they are comprehensive and practical.

7. **Plan for Incident Response:** Establish clear protocols for responding to data breaches or security incidents. Include timely notification procedures and strategies to mitigate harm.

As we integrate technology more deeply into education, the responsibility to protect the data and privacy of our students becomes increasingly significant.

Chapter 41
Future Trends and
Policy Considerations

As we navigate the ever-changing landscape of educational technology, it's clear that the policies governing its use must not only respond to current trends but also anticipate future developments. This section explores emerging trends in educational technology and the corresponding need for flexible, forward-thinking policy frameworks that can adapt to these evolving challenges and opportunities.

In the thriving suburban community of Maplewood, one school stood out for its progressive approach to education: Maplewood Innovators Academy. Recognized as a pioneer in integrating technology into its curriculum, the school had garnered attention for its dynamic policies and forward-thinking initiatives that aimed to harness the power of digital tools while ensuring the well-being of its students.

At the heart of Maplewood Innovators Academy's success was its commitment to creating a technology-rich learning environment. Principal Davis, and the other school leaders, believed technology could transform education, making it more engaging and accessible. To this end, they implemented a one-to-one device program, ensuring that every student had access to a personal tablet or laptop. These devices were equipped with a suite of educational apps and software, enabling students to explore subjects in interactive and innovative ways.

Understanding that technology was constantly evolving, the school's administration developed policies that were both flexible and inclusive. Instead of rigidly adhering to a single approach, they regularly reviewed and updated their policies to incorporate the latest advancements in educational technology. They also prioritized inclusivity, ensuring that all students, regardless of their background or abilities, could benefit from the digital tools available.

For example, they introduced assistive technologies like screen readers and speech-to-text software to support students with disabilities. Additionally, the school's policies emphasized the importance of digital literacy, teaching students how to use technology responsibly and ethically. This comprehensive approach ensured that all students were equipped to navigate the digital world safely and effectively.

One of the hallmarks of Maplewood Innovators Academy was its emphasis on creating dynamic learning experiences. The school adopted a project-based learning model, where students worked on interdisciplinary projects that required them to use various digital tools. These projects not only fostered collaboration and critical thinking but also allowed students to apply their knowledge in real-world contexts.

For instance, in a recent project, students worked on designing sustainable city models using computer-aided design (CAD) software. They researched renewable energy sources, planned urban layouts, and even simulated environmental impacts using digital tools. This project culminated in a virtual presentation to local government officials, showcasing the students' innovative solutions to real-world problems.

Principal Davis understood that the success of technology integration depended on the support and training of educators. To this end, the school invested heavily in professional development. Teachers attended workshops and training sessions on the latest educational technologies and pedagogical strategies. They also had access to a dedicated tech support team that provided ongoing assistance and resources.

Moreover, the school fostered a culture of collaboration among its staff. Teachers met regularly to share best practices, discuss challenges, and brainstorm new ideas. This collaborative spirit extended beyond the school, as Maplewood Innovators Academy formed partnerships with local businesses and universities to stay at the forefront of educational innovation.

Maplewood Innovators Academy's commitment to dynamic and innovative policies set it apart as a leader in educational technology. By continuously adapting to the evolving digital landscape, the school ensured that its students were not only tech-savvy but also prepared to thrive in a rapidly changing world. Principal Davis often said, "Our goal is to empower our students to be the architects of their own futures, equipped with the knowledge and skills to navigate the challenges and opportunities of the digital age."

This story of Maplewood Innovators Academy exemplifies how forward-thinking policies and a commitment to inclusivity can transform education. By embracing the potential of technology and continuously evolving to meet new challenges, schools can create enriching and empowering learning environments for all students.

Emerging Trends in Educational Technology

Staying abreast of emerging trends is crucial for educators, policymakers, and stakeholders. As new technologies continue to transform the classroom experience, they bring both opportunities and challenges that must be thoughtfully addressed. This section explores several key trends shaping the future of education, emphasizing the need for informed and adaptive policies to ensure these advancements enhance learning outcomes and maintain equity and security.

1. **Artificial Intelligence (AI) and Personalized Learning:** AI's potential in creating personalized learning experiences for students is immense. Policies must address how AI can be used ethically and effectively, ensuring it enhances learning without compromising student autonomy or privacy.

2. **Virtual and Augmented Reality:** Immersive technologies like VR and AR are beginning to find their place in classrooms, offering experiential learning opportunities. Policies must consider the implications of these technologies, including content standards, safety, and equitable access.

3. **The Internet of Things (IoT) in Education:** IoT refers to the network of physical devices embedded with sensors, software, and other technologies to connect and exchange data with other devices and systems over the Internet. As IoT devices become more prevalent, they offer opportunities for interactive and connected classrooms. Policy considerations must include data security and network infrastructure to support these advanced technologies.

4. **Blockchain in Education:** Emerging uses of blockchain technology, such as in credentialing and student record management, require policies to address data security, validation processes, and the interoperability of educational records.

The integration of emerging technologies such as AI, VR/AR, IoT, and blockchain in education has the potential to revolutionize learning experiences, making them more personalized, immersive, and efficient. However, the successful implementation of these technologies relies heavily on the development of robust policies that prioritize ethical use, data security, and equitable access. By understanding and addressing these considerations, we can harness the full potential of these innovations to create a more dynamic, inclusive, and forward-thinking educational environment.

The Need for Flexible and Forward-Thinking Policies

The rapid evolution of technology necessitates educational policies that are both flexible and forward-thinking. Anticipatory policy design is essential. It allows policymakers to stay ahead of technological trends and their potential implications in education. Regular review mechanisms ensure these policies remain relevant amidst constant technological advancements. Engaging diverse stakeholders, and including educators, technology experts, students, and parents, leads to more comprehensive and practical policies. Balancing innovation with regulation fosters a safe, progressive learning environment. Additionally, global collaboration in policy development promotes consistent and effective standards worldwide which benefits the global educational community.

Key Aspects:

1. **Anticipatory Policy Design**: Policymakers must adopt a forward-looking approach, anticipating future trends and challenges. This includes staying informed about technological advancements and considering their potential educational applications and implications.

2. **Adaptability and Review Mechanisms**: Policies should be designed with built-in mechanisms for regular review and adaptation. This ensures that they remain relevant and effective in the face of rapid technological changes.

3. **Stakeholder Involvement**: Engaging a broad range of stakeholders

in the policymaking process ensures diverse perspectives and needs are considered. Include educators, technology experts, students, and parents when making policies. This collaborative approach can lead to more comprehensive and practical policies.

4. **Balancing Innovation and Regulation**: Policies should strike a balance between encouraging innovation in educational technology and maintaining necessary regulatory controls. This balance is crucial to foster a safe, effective learning environment open to technological advancements.

5. **Global Collaboration**: Given the global nature of technology, international collaboration in policy development can lead to more consistent and effective standards across borders which benefits the global educational community.

The future of educational technology presents both exciting opportunities and complex challenges. As such, the policies governing its use need to be as dynamic and innovative as the technology itself. By developing flexible, inclusive, and forward-thinking policies, we can ensure that the integration of technology in education continues to enhance learning experiences while safeguarding the interests and well-being of students.

Chapter 42
Global Perspectives and Collaborative Policies

In our increasingly interconnected world, understanding the global landscape of educational technology policy is crucial. Different countries and regions have adopted unique approaches to integrating technology into education, reflecting their diverse cultural, economic, and educational contexts. This section explores these global perspectives and the benefits of collaborative, cross-border policy initiatives.

Focusing on Educational Technology Policies: A Strategic Approach

When a country embarks on the journey of integrating technology into its educational system, it must carefully decide on its priorities and focus areas. The process of selecting what to focus on typically involves several key considerations:

1. **Assessment of Current Needs and Challenges**: The first step is to conduct a thorough assessment of the current state of education within the country. This involves identifying gaps in access to technology,

areas where students are underperforming, and specific challenges faced by teachers and schools. For example, if a country has significant disparities in technology access between urban and rural areas, policies might prioritize equitable distribution of digital resources.

2. **Setting Clear Objectives**: Based on the assessment, the country should set clear and measurable objectives. These could range from improving digital literacy and ensuring equitable access to technology to enhancing teacher training and fostering innovation in teaching methods. For instance, a country like Singapore, which has emphasized innovation and teacher training, might set goals related to professional development and the integration of cutting-edge educational tools.

3. **Engaging Stakeholders**: Effective policymaking involves engaging a wide range of stakeholders, including educators, students, parents, technology experts, and policymakers. By involving these groups, the country can ensure that the policies address the needs and concerns of all parties involved. For example, Estonia's successful integration of digital education involved collaboration between the government, educators, and tech companies to create a cohesive strategy.

4. **Benchmarking Against Best Practices**: Looking at successful models from other countries can provide valuable insights. Countries can benchmark their policies against those of nations that have achieved notable success in integrating technology into education. For instance, Nordic countries' emphasis on equity or the early adoption strategies seen in Estonia can serve as models to emulate or adapt.

5. **Pilot Programs and Phased Implementation**: Before rolling out nationwide policies, it's beneficial to start with pilot programs. These

smaller-scale implementations allow for testing and refinement. By piloting new technologies and teaching methods in select schools or regions, policymakers can gather data on what works and what needs adjustment.

Evaluating the Effectiveness of Educational Technology Policies

Once policies are implemented, it's crucial to evaluate their effectiveness continuously. Here's how countries can gauge whether their strategies are working well:

1. **Data Collection and Analysis**: Regular collection and analysis of data related to student performance, technology usage, and teacher feedback are essential. For instance, tracking improvements in digital literacy scores, graduation rates, or student engagement levels can provide quantitative measures of success.

2. **Feedback Mechanisms**: Establishing feedback loops where educators and students can share their experiences and challenges with the new technologies ensures that policies are responsive and adaptive. Surveys, focus groups, and regular meetings with stakeholders can provide qualitative insights.

3. **Performance Indicators**: Define clear performance indicators that align with the set objectives. These could include metrics such as the number of teachers trained in digital tools, the percentage of schools with high-speed internet access, or student proficiency in digital literacy.

4. **Comparative Studies**: Conduct comparative studies to see how the outcomes of the policies compare with regions or countries with similar demographics but different policies. This can help in understanding the relative effectiveness of the implemented strategies.

5. **External Evaluations**: Engage independent evaluators or international organizations to assess the impact of the policies. External evaluations can provide an unbiased view of the successes and areas needing improvement.

6. **Flexibility and Iteration**: Policies should not be static. Based on the evaluations and feedback, countries should be willing to iterate and refine their strategies. This ongoing process ensures that the policies remain relevant and effective in a rapidly changing technological landscape.

By following these steps, countries can not only implement effective educational technology policies but also ensure that they continuously evolve to meet the needs of their students and educators.

Diverse Approaches in Policymaking

1. **Nordic Countries with an Emphasis on Equity:** Nations like Finland and Sweden prioritize equitable access to technology in education. Their policies focus on ensuring that every student, regardless of background, has access to digital tools and resources, underpinning their strong performance in educational equity.

2. **Singapore's Focus on Innovation and Teacher Training:** Singapore's approach to educational technology is marked by its emphasis

on teacher training and innovation. The government has invested significantly in professional development programs, ensuring that teachers are well-equipped to integrate technology in their classrooms.

3. **United States with Varied State-Level Approaches:** In the US, educational technology policies vary significantly from state to state. Some states have implemented comprehensive digital learning standards and robust funding for technology, while others are still developing their approach.

4. **Estonia's Early Adoption of Digital Education:** Known for its advanced digital infrastructure, Estonia has integrated technology into its educational system from an early stage. Policies support digital literacy from a young age, with a strong focus on coding and computer science.

Benefits of Collaborative and Cross-Border Policy Initiatives

In an interconnected world, the benefits of collaborative and cross-border policy initiatives in educational technology are immense. By working together, countries can share best practices, develop standardized educational technology standards, and address the global digital divide. Such collaboration ensures that technological advancements in education benefit students worldwide, fostering global citizenship and enhancing research and development efforts. This collective approach not only leverages the strengths of each participating nation but also creates a more equitable, effective, and interconnected educational landscape.

1. **Sharing of Best Practices:** International collaboration allows

countries to share best practices and learn from each other's experiences. For example, countries with advanced digital education systems can provide insights and models for others just beginning their journey.

2. **Standardization of Educational Technology Standards:** Collaborative policies can lead to the development of standardized global educational technology standards, making it easier to share resources and collaborate on international education projects.

3. **Addressing the Global Digital Divide:** Joint initiatives can help address the global digital divide, ensuring that advancements in educational technology benefit students worldwide, not just in economically advanced countries.

4. **Fostering Global Citizenship:** Collaborative educational technology policies support the development of global citizenship skills, preparing students to work and thrive in a globalized world.

5. **Research and Development:** Cross-border collaborations can boost research and development in educational technology, leading to innovative solutions tailored to diverse educational needs.

The approach to educational technology policy varies significantly across the globe, reflecting the unique challenges and opportunities each region faces. By adopting a collaborative and cross-border approach to policymaking, countries can leverage each other's strengths, share valuable insights, and work together to create a more equitable, effective, and interconnected educational landscape.

Charting the Course for Future-Ready Education

The integration of technology in education is not just a trend but a fundamental shift in how we approach teaching and learning. For policymakers, there are multifaceted challenges and opportunities that come with this shift. The key takeaways underscore the need for thoughtful, informed, and dynamic policies that can effectively support and shape the future of education.

Key Takeaways for Policymakers

1. **Embrace the Rapid Pace of Technological Change:** Policies need to be adaptable and responsive to keep pace with the rapidly evolving world of educational technology.

2. **Prioritize Equity and Accessibility:** Ensuring equitable access to technology for all students, regardless of their socio-economic background or abilities, is crucial in avoiding a deepened digital divide.

3. **Invest in Teacher Training and Professional Development:** The success of technology integration heavily relies on teachers being well-equipped and confident in using these tools.

4. **Balance Innovation with Pragmatism:** While encouraging innovation, policies should also be grounded in practicality, ensuring they are feasible and sustainable in the long term.

5. **Data Privacy and Security Are Paramount:** As technology becomes more embedded in education, safeguarding student data must be a top priority.

6. **Collaboration Is Key:** Collaborative and cross-border initiatives can enhance the quality and efficacy of educational technology policies, benefiting from shared experiences and expertise.

A Call to Action

To policymakers embarking on this journey, the call to action is clear: Develop and implement policies that not only reflect current technological advancements but also anticipate future trends. Engage with a broad spectrum of stakeholders—from educators and technologists to students and parents—to ensure that these policies are comprehensive, inclusive, and aligned with the broader goals of education.

Foster environments where technology is used not merely as a tool for information delivery but as a catalyst for creativity, problem-solving, and critical thinking. Recognize the potential of technology to transform education but remain mindful of its challenges and pitfalls.

As we stand at this pivotal juncture in educational history, the decisions made by policymakers today will shape the educational landscapes of tomorrow. Let us approach this task with a vision that is both bold and cautious, innovative yet grounded, ensuring that the integration of technology in education opens doors to new possibilities, equips students with essential 21st-century skills, and prepares them to thrive in an increasingly digital world.

Section 8
The Future of Education and Technology

Chapter 43
The Ripple Effect: Empowering the Next Generation

Growing up in the 1990s, my first exposure to technology in the classroom was vastly different from what students experience today. Back then, the sight of a computer lab was enough to make our eyes widen in awe. Our lessons on technology were limited to learning basic computer operations, typing skills, and the occasional educational game. The computers were bulky, the software rudimentary, and the internet, well, it was still in its infancy, characterized by dial-up connections and static-filled modem sounds.

I vividly remember the excitement of logging onto a computer, opening up a program like "Oregon Trail" or "Math Blaster," and navigating through its simplistic yet captivating graphics. These early interactions with technology were exciting, but they were also constrained. The primary focus was on familiarizing ourselves with the hardware and basic software rather than integrating technology seamlessly into our everyday learning.

Fast forward to today, and the landscape has transformed dramatically. Modern classrooms are equipped with sleek laptops, tablets, interactive whiteboards, and high-speed internet. The tools available to students are not just about learning to use technology but also about using technology to learn. This shift is profound and has fueled my passion for ensuring that today's students are equipped with the tools and skills they need to thrive in an ever-changing technological world.

In today's classrooms, students are creating digital stories, programming robots, collaborating on cloud-based platforms, and diving into virtual reality experiences. The focus has shifted from merely understanding technology to leveraging it as a powerful tool for creativity, critical thinking, and problem-solving. The iTECH model exemplifies this shift, encouraging students to explore, create, and collaborate using a variety of digital tools.

My journey from those early computer labs to the tech-rich environments we see today has underscored the importance of adapting to technological advancements. It's not about keeping up with the latest gadgets; it's about preparing students for a future where technology will play an integral role in every aspect of their lives. This passion drives me to advocate for a community of empowered educators who can collectively ignite a flame of curiosity and innovation in our students.

The phrase "it takes a village" resonates deeply when we consider the holistic development of students. By creating a community of empowered educators, we do more than enhance our own teaching methodologies: we ignite a flame that extends far beyond the confines of the classroom. This ripple effect, this profound influence, has the potential to shape the future of education and the learners within it. As someone who has witnessed the evolution of educational technology firsthand, I am committed to ensuring that our students have the tools and support they need to navigate and thrive in this digital age.

Empowered Educators Inspire Proactive Learners

When educators are well-supported, continually learning, and excited about their craft, it's palpable. Students can sense this passion and enthusiasm. This energy isn't just infectious—it's transformative in several ways.

1. **Modeling Lifelong Learning:** As educators actively engage in professional development and community-building, they exemplify the values of lifelong learning. This can inspire students to view education as a continuous journey, not just a series of exams.

   - Mr. Thompson, a high school science teacher, regularly attends workshops and online courses to stay updated with the latest scientific discoveries and educational technologies. His students notice his enthusiasm for learning new things, and it encourages them to adopt a similar attitude. One day, Mr. Thompson excitedly shares insights from a recent workshop on renewable energy. His passion and commitment to continuous learning inspire the class to explore topics beyond the curriculum. This fosters a culture of curiosity and intellectual growth.

2. **Encouraging Autonomy:** Empowered educators, having benefited from collaboration and autonomy in their learning paths, are more likely to encourage similar independence in their students. This can foster a sense of agency in learners, making them more proactive in seeking knowledge.

   - Ms. Williams, an elementary school teacher, values the autonomy she experiences through professional development and collaborative teaching. She transfers this autonomy to her students by implementing project-based learning, where students choose their projects and work at their own pace. For instance, during a history unit, students select a historical event to research and present. This independence helps the class develop self-direction and confidence. This makes them proactive learners who take responsibility for their education.

3. **Fostering a Growth Mindset:** Teachers who continuously refine their craft through community input and learning opportunities often

adopt a growth mindset. When students witness this adaptability and resilience in their educators, they, too, are more likely to embrace challenges and view failures as learning opportunities. A growth mindset is the belief that abilities and intelligence can be developed through dedication, hard work, and learning. This mindset contrasts with a fixed mindset, which assumes that abilities are static and unchangeable. Embracing a growth mindset encourages individuals to embrace challenges, persevere through setbacks, see effort as a path to mastery, and learn from criticism. It also fosters a love of learning and resilience, which are essential for achieving personal and academic growth.

- Mrs. Carter, a middle school math teacher, continually refines her teaching methods by engaging with a community of educators. She openly discusses her challenges and successes with her students, demonstrating resilience and a growth mindset. When a student struggles with a math problem, Mrs. Carter shares her own experiences of overcoming difficulties and encourages the student to see mistakes as learning opportunities. This approach helps students develop a positive attitude toward challenges, understanding that perseverance leads to improvement and success.

Long-term Benefits of a Community-Driven Approach

The ripple effects of a community-driven educational approach are vast and enduring. Research has indicated that students benefit cognitively from educators who engage in continuous professional development.[11] Such teachers are more likely to employ innovative teaching strategies that cater

11   Linda Darling-Hammond and Milbrey W. McLaughlin, "Policies That Support Professional Development in an Era of Reform," *Phi Delta Kappan* 76, no. 8 (1995): 597–604.

to various learning styles, leading to better student outcomes.

In a rapidly changing world, students need more than rote learning. They require critical thinking, adaptability, and collaborative skills. A community-driven approach, which emphasizes these values among educators, ensures students are better prepared for the challenges of tomorrow.

Students of empowered educators benefit not just academically but also emotionally and socially.[12] When teachers collaborate and support each other, they create positive learning environments that nurture students' emotional well-being and social skills.

The ripples created by a community of empowered educators can touch every facet of a student's life. As educators, the drive to better ourselves, to collaborate, and to embrace community isn't merely for our benefit—it's a gift we pass on, a legacy that has the potential to shape generations to come.

The Strength of the Collective

Just as we teach our students the significance of teamwork and collaboration, we, too, as educators, must remember that our collective wisdom, experiences, and passion far surpass what we bring individually. Through sharing, discussing, and even debating, we refine our methods, discover new tools, and most importantly, support one another in a field that is as challenging as it is rewarding.

Being part of a community isn't just about taking—it's about giving. By contributing our unique perspectives, solutions, and questions, we enrich the tapestry of this collective journey. Whether it's joining an online group, attending seminars, or simply initiating a discussion in the teachers' lounge, every action, no matter how small, fosters this sense of community.

So, consider this a beginning—a call to dive deeper into the vast sea

---

12 Patricia A. Jennings and Mark T. Greenberg, "The Prosocial Classroom: Teacher Social and Emotional Competence in Relation to Student and Classroom Outcomes," *Review of Educational Research* 79, no. 1 (2009): 491–525.

of educational technology with the strength of a community by your side. Seek out networks, share your insights, ask questions, and most importantly, remember that every educator, from the novice to the expert, has something valuable to offer.

In the words of Helen Keller, "Alone we can do so little; together we can do so much." In the ever-evolving world of EdTech, let's commit to doing "so much" together for the benefit of ourselves, our peers, and most importantly, our students.

Chapter 44
Embracing Change in the Educational Landscape

As we reach a pivotal moment in this exploration of the evolving educational landscape, one truth resonates above all: change is not just inevitable; it is already upon us. The educational realm has been undergoing a transformation of unprecedented scale, primarily driven by the rapid integration of digital technology. This shift towards digital integration marks a significant turn in how education is delivered, experienced, and perceived.

The Rapid Evolution of Educational Landscapes

The classrooms of today bear little resemblance to those of a mere decade ago. Digital blackboards have replaced chalkboards. Tablets and laptops have taken over from notebooks and textbooks, and the vast expanse of the internet has opened up limitless possibilities for learning and exploration. This evolution is not merely about the introduction of new tools; it's about a fundamental shift in the approach to education—a shift from a teacher-centered model to a more student-centric, interactive, and collaborative approach.

Digital integration in education has gone beyond the superficial use of gadgets and entered a realm where technology is fundamentally altering the pedagogical process. We've witnessed how models like the iTECH model have transformed classrooms into dynamic learning environments where creativity, problem-solving, and critical thinking skills are at the forefront. Technology is no longer an add-on or a luxury; it has become an integral part of the curriculum, necessary for providing students with the skills and knowledge they need in the 21st century.

Adapting to Meet the Needs for Digital Literacy

The transition to a digitally integrated educational system brings with it an imperative need: the need for digital literacy. It's not enough for students to merely have access to technology; they must also be equipped with the skills to use it effectively and responsibly. Digital literacy encompasses understanding how to navigate the online world, critically evaluate information, maintain cybersecurity, and use digital tools for learning and problem-solving.

Educators, too, must adapt to this changing landscape. The roles of teachers are evolving, requiring them to be facilitators, guides, and co-learners in the digital journey alongside their students. This necessitates ongoing professional development and a commitment to lifelong learning, ensuring educators are equipped to guide their students through the digital world effectively.

As we reflect on the journey through the chapters of this book, it becomes clear that embracing the changes in the educational landscape is not just about keeping up with technology. Rather, it's about re-envisioning the way we educate. It's about preparing our students for a future where technology and digital literacy will be intertwined with every aspect of their personal and professional lives. The shift towards digital integration is a call to action for all involved in education to adapt, grow, and thrive in this new and exciting digital era.

A Recap of the iTECH Model

Throughout the previous chapters, we have dissected and discussed the iTECH model in detail, a revolutionary approach that exemplifies the paradigm shift in modern education. This model, standing at the forefront of educational transformation, encapsulates the transition from traditional teaching methods to a more dynamic, technology-integrated approach. Let us recapitulate its core concepts and explore how it aligns with the current and future directions of education.

Core Phases of the iTECH model

1. **Inspire:** The iTECH model begins with inspiration, where educators ignite curiosity and interest in their students, not just presenting them with information but engaging them in the joy of discovery.

2. **Try:** This stage encourages students to experiment with new technologies, fostering a hands-on approach to learning. It's about exploration, making mistakes, and learning from them, which is critical in developing problem-solving skills.

3. **Expand:** Here, the focus is on expanding knowledge and understanding. It's where educators and students delve deeper into concepts, leveraging technology to enhance learning and comprehension.

4. **Create:** In the Create phase, students apply their learning to build

something new. This phase is about using technology for creation and encouraging creativity and innovation.

5. **Huddle:** Finally, the Huddle phase emphasizes collaboration and feedback. Students and teachers come together to share, discuss, and refine their creations, fostering a sense of community and collaborative learning.

Alignment with Current and Future Educational Needs

The iTECH model aligns seamlessly with the current needs and future directions of education in several ways:

1. **Emphasis on 21st-Century Skills and Beyond:** In an era where critical thinking, creativity, and digital literacy are paramount, the iTECH model fosters these skills through its interactive and technology-driven approach.

2. **Personalized Learning:** The model supports personalized learning, as technology can be used to cater to the individual learning styles and paces of students, a crucial aspect in today's diverse educational landscape.

3. **Preparation for a Digital Future:** With its focus on technology integration, the iTECH model prepares students for a future where digital proficiency is essential.

4. **Fostering Lifelong Learning:** By encouraging exploration, creation, and collaboration, the iTECH model instills a love for learning that transcends the classroom, preparing students to be lifelong learners.

5. **Adaptability and Flexibility:** The model is adaptable and can be tailored to fit various educational settings and curricula, making it a versatile tool in the evolving world of education.

The iTECH model is more than just a method; it is a reflection of where education is headed. It is a comprehensive approach that responds to the current educational needs and paves the way for future learning paradigms. By embracing this model, educators and institutions are not just adapting to change. They are leading it, ensuring that students are equipped, empowered, and inspired to thrive in an increasingly digital world.

A Call to Action for Educators

As we stand at the cusp of a new era in education, a clarion call goes out to educators everywhere. The integration of the iTECH model and educational technology into your teaching practices is not just an opportunity; it's an imperative. It's a journey that requires courage, creativity, and a commitment to continual learning, but the rewards—enhanced student engagement, improved learning outcomes, and preparation of students for a digital future—are immeasurable.

Embracing the iTECH Model

1. **Start with Inspiration:** Reflect on your teaching practices. Ask yourself, "How can I inspire curiosity and a love for learning in this digital age?" Use technology as a medium to spark imagination and creativity.

2. **Experiment and Explore:** Don't be afraid to try new technologies. Whether it's a new app, a digital platform, or an interactive software,

give yourself the freedom to experiment. Remember, every great innovation in education began with a willingness to explore.

3. **Expand Your Knowledge:** Stay informed about the latest trends in educational technology. Attend workshops, webinars, and conferences. Network with fellow educators to learn about their experiences with technology in the classroom.

4. **Create and Innovate:** Use technology to create new learning experiences. This could be anything from integrating a game-based learning platform into your lesson plan to using virtual reality for a history lesson.

5. **Collaborate and Share:** The final phase of the iTECH model, Huddle, is about collaboration. Share your experiences, successes, and challenges with your peers. Collaborate with other educators to create a rich, supportive learning community.

Actionable Steps for Educators

1. **Set Clear Goals:** Begin by setting clear and achievable goals for integrating technology into your teaching. It could be as simple as using a digital tool for assessments or incorporating multimedia into your lectures.

2. **Leverage Available Resources:** Utilize the resources your school or district provides. If there are limitations, look for free or low-cost online resources that can supplement your teaching.

3. **Foster a Growth Mindset:** Cultivate a growth mindset, both in yourself and in your students. Encourage risk-taking, experimentation, and learning from failures.

4. **Seek Support:** If you're unsure where to start, seek support from your school's technology coordinator or a tech-savvy colleague. Mentorship can be a powerful tool on this journey.

5. **Reflect and Adapt:** Continuously reflect on your experiences with educational technology. Be open to adapting your approaches based on what works best for your students.

The journey into integrating the iTECH model and educational technology into your teaching practices is a path of transformation for both you and your students. It's a path that leads to a more engaging, dynamic, and relevant education. As educators, we have the power to shape the future of learning and to inspire a new generation of creative thinkers and problem solvers. Embrace this journey with an open heart and mind, and watch as the world of education transforms before your eyes.

Chapter 45
A Vision for the Future

In a high school in California, a project-based learning initiative integrated technology across various subjects. Students used digital tools to research, design, and implement solutions to real-world problems. This approach not only fostered creativity. It also honed their research and critical thinking skills as they evaluated data and presented their findings using digital platforms.

A middle school in Sweden introduced coding into their curriculum across various subjects. By learning to code, students developed logical thinking and problem-solving skills. Projects like creating simple apps or games encouraged both creative and computational thinking.

A school in Australia used virtual reality (VR) to bring history lessons to life. Students explored ancient civilizations in a 3D environment, which not only made learning more engaging but also encouraged them to ask in-depth questions, analyze historical contexts, and think critically about the past.

The integration of technology in education is a gateway to developing the creative and critical thinking skills that are indispensable in the 21st century. By leveraging digital tools, educators can provide learning experiences that are not only more engaging and relevant but also conducive to building the higher-order thinking skills that students need to navigate an increasingly complex world. In this journey, the role of educators is crucial—as facilitators and guides who open the doors to new ways of thinking and learning.

Inspiring Creative and Critical Thinkers

The integration of technology is about redefining the way we approach problem-solving, creativity, and critical thinking. This section delves into how technology, when integrated thoughtfully into education, can be a powerful catalyst for developing creative and critical thinkers.

The infusion of digital tools in education opens up a universe of possibilities for creative expression and innovation. Technology provides students with diverse mediums to express their ideas, be it through digital storytelling, coding projects, video production, or interactive presentations. This variety not only engages students but also encourages them to think outside the conventional boundaries of text and paper.

Digital technology also plays a pivotal role in enhancing critical thinking skills. Online resources, simulations, and interactive platforms offer students opportunities to analyze information, solve complex problems, and make informed decisions. The Internet, a vast reservoir of information, challenges students to evaluate the credibility of sources, understand varying perspectives, and synthesize information—all key components of critical thinking.

Empowering Students for Future Success

In a world where digital fluency is as essential as reading and writing, technology-enhanced education is a launchpad for future success in a variety of careers and life pursuits. This section explores how integrating technology into education prepares students for the challenges and opportunities of the future and the vital role educators play in this journey.

In an age where technology permeates every aspect of our lives, from personal interactions to professional environments, students who are digitally fluent—who can navigate, understand, and utilize technology effectively—are at a distinct advantage. Technology-enhanced education develops these competencies, preparing students for the realities of the modern workforce.

The use of technology in education helps students develop a range of skills. They include digital literacy, critical thinking, problem-solving, and adaptability. These skills are highly valued in virtually all career paths and are crucial for navigating the complexities of the 21st-century workplace and beyond.

As team-based and remote work becomes increasingly common in professional settings, technology in education teaches students how to collaborate and communicate effectively in digital environments. Tools like collaborative platforms and virtual meeting software have become familiar, easing the transition into the modern workplace.

The Role of Educators in Guiding Effective Technology Use

Educators play a crucial role in modeling and teaching responsible and ethical use of technology. This includes understanding digital citizenship, respecting intellectual property, and being mindful of digital footprints.

Educators are tasked with more than just introducing technology; they must integrate it in a way that enhances learning and aligns with curriculum goals. This involves selecting appropriate technological tools and strategies that support the learning objectives and cater to the diverse needs of students.

It's important for educators to teach students not just to use technology but to critically engage with it. This means encouraging students to question and analyze the information they encounter online and understand the biases and limitations of digital platforms.

The future is inherently unpredictable, particularly in terms of technological advancement. Educators can prepare students for this uncertainty by fostering a mindset of lifelong learning and adaptability, ensuring they are ready to learn and evolve with the changing technological landscape.

The integration of technology in education is a critical factor in preparing students for their future academic and career endeavors. By developing digital fluency and adaptable skill sets, and with the guidance of educators, students are both prepared to meet the challenges of their future careers and equipped to be responsible, informed citizens in a digital world.

Long-term Impact on Education and Society

As we venture deeper into the 21st century, the long-term impacts of a technology-empowered education system begin to crystallize, revealing profound implications for both individual students and society at large. This section examines these potential impacts and speculates on the future trends and developments in digital literacy education.

Impacts on Individual Students

The integration of technology in education profoundly influences individual students, shaping their future in multiple ways. By enhancing employability, students gain a competitive edge in the digital job market through familiarity with essential tools and skills. Furthermore, technology fosters a culture of lifelong learning, encouraging students to continuously seek knowledge and adapt to new challenges. Finally, global connectivity enabled by technology breaks down geographical barriers, exposing students to diverse perspectives and preparing them to thrive in an interconnected world. The following sections explore these individual impacts in detail.

1. **Enhanced Employability:** In an increasingly digital job market, students emerging from a technology-rich educational background will have a competitive edge. Their familiarity with digital tools and platforms, coupled with critical thinking and problem-solving skills honed through technology use, makes them highly employable.

2. **Lifelong Learning:** Exposure to technology in education fosters a culture of lifelong learning. With continuous access to online resources and learning platforms, students are more likely to continue their education beyond formal schooling, adapting to new skills and knowledge as required in their professional and personal lives.

3. **Global Connectivity:** Technology-empowered education breaks down geographical barriers, exposing students to global perspectives and networks. This connectivity not only enriches their educational experience. It also prepares them to operate in a globally interconnected world.

Impacts on Society

The integration of technology in education extends its influence beyond the classroom, significantly impacting society. When executed equitably, it can bridge socio-economic divides by providing quality resources to underserved communities. This democratization of education not only fosters innovation and economic growth by creating a tech-savvy workforce but also promotes informed citizenship. Digital literacy equips individuals with the skills to engage with contemporary issues, participate in democratic processes, and contribute meaningfully to societal discourse. The following sections delve into these profound societal impacts.

1. **Bridging Socio-Economic Divides:** If implemented equitably, technology in education has the potential to level the playing field, providing high-quality educational resources and opportunities to

traditionally underserved communities, thereby reducing socio-economic disparities.

2. **Fostering Innovation and Economic Growth:** An education system that emphasizes digital literacy and technology use can stimulate innovation. A workforce skilled in these areas is a critical driver of economic growth, particularly in sectors reliant on technological advancement.

3. **Promoting Informed Citizenship:** Digital literacy is crucial for understanding and engaging with contemporary issues. An informed citizenry, adept at navigating and analyzing digital information, is better equipped to participate in democratic processes and societal discourse.

Future Trends and Developments in Digital Literacy Education

It's impossible to predict all future technologies. However, the iTECH model equips students with the skills to adapt to any technological advancements, ensuring they can navigate and utilize new tools effectively.

1. **Artificial Intelligence and Personalized Learning:** AI is poised to play a significant role in personalizing education as it adapts learning experiences to the needs, abilities, and interests of individual students.

2. **Immersive Learning Experiences:** Technologies like virtual reality (VR) and augmented reality (AR) will likely become more prevalent, offering students immersive and interactive learning experiences that were previously impossible.

3. **Focus on Data Ethics and Cybersecurity:** As reliance on digital

tools increases, education in data ethics and cybersecurity will become more integral, equipping students with the skills to navigate the digital world safely and ethically.

4. **Blended Learning Environments:** The future will likely see a more seamless integration of in-person and online learning, with technology enabling a more flexible, hybrid approach to education.

The trajectory of technology-empowered education points toward a future where digital literacy is interwoven into the fabric of learning. Its long-term impacts on students and society are profound, paving the way for a more equitable, innovative, and interconnected world. As educators and policymakers, the task at hand is not just to adapt to these changes but to proactively shape them to ensure the educational systems of tomorrow are inclusive, effective, and forward-looking.

We stand at a pivotal moment in history. The integration of technology in education is more than a fleeting trend; it's a fundamental shift in how we teach, learn, and interact. This shift ushers in a vision of the future where education is not just about imparting knowledge. Instead, it's about empowering learners with the skills, tools, and mindset to navigate and shape an increasingly digital world.

Imagine a future where classrooms are no longer confined by four walls but are connected hubs of learning, offering limitless resources and opportunities for collaboration across the globe. Education is personalized and adaptive, catering to the unique needs and learning styles of each student. Technology is seamlessly integrated, not as a mere adjunct but as a core aspect of the educational experience, enhancing creativity, critical thinking, and problem-solving skills.

In this vision, educators are not just conveyors of knowledge but facilitators and guides in a journey of discovery and exploration. They are empowered with the tools and training to effectively harness technology, fostering an environment of continual learning and innovation.

The Role of Educators, Policymakers, and Stakeholders

The role of educators in this future is critical. It requires a commitment to continual learning and adaptation, embracing new technologies and pedagogies to create engaging and effective learning experiences. Educators must also be mentors and role models in digital literacy, guiding students to use technology responsibly and ethically.

For policymakers, this future demands foresight, flexibility, and a commitment to creating and supporting policies that anticipate future challenges and opportunities. It's about building infrastructures that support equitable access to technology, ensuring every student, regardless of their background, has the opportunity to succeed in a digital world.

Stakeholders in education, including parents, community members, and industry partners, all play a vital role in shaping the future of education. Collaboration and partnership among these stakeholders are essential in providing students with the resources, opportunities, and support they need to thrive.

As we move forward, the call to action is clear: embrace change, innovate with purpose, and commit to a lifelong journey of learning and adaptation. The future of education in a digital world is not a distant dream; it's a reality we are shaping today. By working together, we can ensure this future is bright, equitable, and full of possibilities for every learner.

The Technology Toolbox for Teachers

As technology evolves, the challenge of keeping up with the latest tools and their applications in the classroom becomes more significant. To address this, I invite you to join my "Technology Toolbox for Teachers" subscription membership. This resource offers a comprehensive collection of user-friendly tutorials for over 120 popular tech tools, ensuring you remain at the forefront of educational innovation.

By subscribing, you'll gain access to:

1. **In-Depth Tutorials**: Easy-to-follow guides that help you master a variety of tech tools, whether you are a novice or an experienced user.

2. **Creative Ideas for Classroom Use**: A wealth of innovative ideas tailored for engaging elementary students, sparking creativity, and enhancing learning experiences.

3. **Regular Updates**: Stay current with the latest educational technologies as our library is continuously updated with new tools and resources.

4. **Professional Development Support**: Lead professional development sessions with confidence using our tutorials and ready-made presentations, helping your colleagues benefit from your expertise.

The "Technology Toolbox for Teachers" is designed with educators in mind, providing everything from basic introductions to advanced tutorials, all aimed at making your teaching more effective and exciting. Join us today and transform your classroom into a hub of digital innovation.

For more information and to subscribe, scan the QR code.

About the Author

Brittany Washburn is an educational technology specialist, curriculum developer, and advocate for empowering teachers to integrate technology with confidence and purpose. With over a decade of experience teaching computer science and digital literacy, Brittany has inspired thousands of educators to approach technology not as an obstacle, but as a bridge to deeper learning and creativity. Her work centers on helping students become critical thinkers, problem solvers, and responsible digital citizens prepared for the challenges of the 21st century.

As the creator of the *K-5 Technology Curriculum* and *Technology Toolbox for Teachers*, Brittany has built a robust suite of digital learning resources used in classrooms around the world. Her innovative curriculum design and practical approach to technology integration have been recognized for their impact and effectiveness. Her resources have been featured across prominent educational platforms and blogs, where she continues to help shape the conversation around modern digital learning.

Brittany has presented at numerous conferences, including STEM CON, Teach Your Heart Out, TCEA, and the Canopy EdTech Conference. Her sessions blend strategy and inspiration, providing educators with actionable tools to bring digital learning to life in every classroom. She developed the iTECH Model, a framework designed to guide teachers through integrating technology in ways that foster creativity, collaboration, and critical thinking.

At the heart of Brittany's work is a vision for the next generation. To empower students to become content creators instead of passive consumers.

The Digital Classroom reflects this mission by equipping teachers with the strategies and confidence to transform students from users of technology into innovators who shape the world through it. She believes that when educators model creativity and curiosity, students learn to use technology not just to access information, but to imagine, build, and lead.

Everything EdTech Series

The AI Classroom
By Daniel Fitzpatrick, Amanda Fox, and Brad Weinstein

Step into the future of teaching with *The AI Classroom*, your essential guide to understanding and embracing artificial intelligence in education. This forward-thinking book shows how AI can empower teachers, personalize learning, and save valuable time, all while keeping humanity at the heart of innovation. Learn to harness AI tools to create inclusive, engaging, and future-ready classrooms.

Modern PBL
By Daniel Jones

Empower your students to become creators, innovators, and problem-solvers with *Modern PBL*. This transformative guide redefines Project-Based Learning for today's digital world, where curiosity fuels discovery and technology enhances authentic learning. Discover how to design experiences that challenge students to think critically, collaborate meaningfully, and rise above AI-driven shortcuts.

Bulk Orders

TeacherGoals Publishing, LLC offers bulk orders for any of our titles. A minimum of 25 copies must be ordered for bulk orders, and orders qualify for discounts. You can also request information about signed copies, book studies, and more. Scan the QR code for more information.